THE AUTHOR

Rosemary Conley is the UK's leading diet and fitness expert. Her diet and fitness books and videos have consistently topped the bestseller lists with combined sales in excess of nine million copies. Rosemary has also presented more than 250 cookery programmes on TV. In 2001 Rosemary was made an Honorary Freeman of the City of Leicester, and in 2004 she was awarded a CBE for services to the fitness and diet industries.

Together with her husband, Mike Rimmington, Rosemary runs four companies: Rosemary Conley Diet and Fitness Clubs, which operates a national network of almost 200 franchises running over 2,000 classes weekly; Quorn House Publishing Ltd, which publishes *Rosemary Conley Diet & Fitness magazine*; Rosemary Conley Licences Ltd; and Rosemary Conley Enterprises.

Rosemary Conley's
Gi Jeans Diet

Gi made easy – the all new diet plan

arrow books

Published by Century in 2006

5 7 9 10 8 6

First published in the United Kingdom in 2006 by Arrow
Random House UK Limited
20 Vauxhall Bridge Road, London SW1V 2SA

Random House Australia (Pty) Limited
20 Alfred Street, Milsons Point, Sydney,
New South Wales 2061, Australia

Random House New Zealand Limited
18 Poland Road, Glenfield, Auckland 10, New Zealand

Random House South Africa (Pty) Limited
Isle of Houghton, Corner of Boundary Road & Carse O'Gowrie
Houghton 2198, South Africa

Random House UK Limited Reg. No. 954009

A CIP catalogue record for this book is available
from the British Library

Papers used by Random House UK Limited are natural, recyclable products made from wood grown in sustainable forests. The manufacturing processes conform to the environmental regulations of the country of origin

ISBN 009 949 2571

Cover photograph by Alan Olley
Edited by Jan Bowmer
Designed by Roger Walker

Printed and bound in Great Britain by
Bookmarque Ltd, Croydon, Surrey

Acknowledgments

I have thoroughly enjoyed writing this book and I hope it helps you succeed in achieving a slim and fit body. I surround myself with experts in my work and I have the pleasure of working with some very special people who are far more technically knowledgeable than I am. I know that my readers want to learn how to lose weight and get fitter, healthily and safely, and I hope that I have put that knowledge into understandable language that will also motivate them into action.

For the last 12 years I have had the real privilege of working with Mary Morris, M.Sc., who heads our training department for Rosemary Conley Diet and Fitness Clubs. Mary has choreographed all my fitness videos and DVDs during that time and we have enormous fun working together. The fitness programmes and the fitness quiz included in this book have been created by Mary. Thank you, Mary, for your tremendous support and continued contribution and interest in my work.

Dr Susan Jebb is an eminent nutrition scientist as well as Chair of the Association for the Study of Obesity. Thank you so much, Susan, for your encouragement and invaluable guidance with this book.

I would like to thank Julie Mayer from Radio Leicester, who so enthusiastically launched the Diet Trial which enabled my GI

Jeans Diet to be tested by her listeners before I wrote this book. Thank you also to my Trial Dieters.

My PA for the last 11 years is Melody Patterson, who has worked extremely hard in bringing the various chapters of this book into some kind of order as well as calculating the nutrient content of all the menus and recipes. Thank you, Melody, for all your support and hard work.

I also want to give enormous thanks to my editor Jan Bowmer for making my manuscript into the book it is today. Your expertise and enthusiasm for what I do, and your interest and attention to detail, are very much appreciated.

Thank you also to chef Dean Simpole-Clarke for compiling the delicious recipes in this book. I hope they will help everyone who follows this programme to feel that it isn't like a diet at all but more a delicious way of eating.

I also want to say a huge thank you to my daughter, Dawn, who acted as my assistant when I went away to write this book. Your wisdom in knowing what my dieters want from me and your encouragement to 'stick at it' is appreciated more than you realise.

Many thanks also to Roger Walker, who has designed this book, and to my husband, Mike, for his total support, patience and love throughout the writing of this book.

Thank you all.

Useful information

Weight conversions

Ounce (oz)	Pound (lb)	Gram (g)
1		25
2		50
3		75
4	¼	115
6		175
8	½	225
16	1	450
	1½	675
	2	1kg

Liquid measures

15ml	=	½fl oz	
30ml	=	1fl oz	
50ml	=	2fl oz	
75ml	=	2½fl oz	
120ml	=	4fl oz	
150ml	=		¼ pint
175ml	=	6fl oz	
250ml	=	8fl oz	
300ml	=		½ pint
400ml	=	14fl oz	
450ml	=		¾ pint
600ml	=		1 pint
1.2 litres	=		2 pints

Abbreviations and symbols used

oz	ounce
lb	pound
g	gram
kg	kilogram
st	stone
fl oz	fluid ounce
ml	millilitre
kcal	calories
tsp	teaspoon
tbsp	tablespoon
Ⓥ	suitable for vegetarians
❄	suitable for home freezing

Contents

1 It really, really works!

My Gi Jeans Diet works. It really, really works! You will lose weight fast but healthily and, remarkably, you will not feel hungry because the whole principle of the Gi way of eating is to eat foods that are slowly digested and absorbed, which helps you feel fuller for longer. Not only will you see sensational results faster than ever before, you will also be giving your body the best possible health boost.

I have read several of the recent rush of Gi diets that have been published and I was not only surprised at how confusing they were but, most of all, at how complicated they appeared. I felt that having to learn the Gi ratings of thousands of foods as well as count calories AND watch out for fat content was a step too far for the average in-a-rush dieter. So on that basis I set myself a challenge to come up with a weight-reducing diet that was simple to follow but Gi-based, low in fat, and calorie counted.

Gi has brought a new perspective to dieting, but the principles of weight loss remain unchanged. My goal was to create an eating plan that would be ultra-healthy and Gi-based, one that would work quickly and effectively in reducing weight and inches. I then had to add a fitness plan which would speed up the rate of weight loss and significantly improve fitness levels, one that dieters would find easy to stick with in the future. Losing weight and getting fit for the short term is a waste of time. It has to be a long-term lifestyle modification programme.

As soon as I started to put the diet together I went on local radio and asked for volunteers to try out the diet. The response was brilliant. From the dozens of volunteers, five trial dieters were selected to appear on Radio Leicester for a live weigh-in every couple of weeks, and their results and comments are included in chapter 18. Julie Mayer, the lunchtime presenter, who selected the 'famous five' for her new 'Flab Fighters' slot wasn't disappointed with their performance. In the first two weeks their individual weight losses ranged from 5½lb to 12lb and, at the end of the eight-week trial, from 1st 3lb to 2st 1lb, making a total loss of 4st 5½lb! The two men and three women team also attended my own diet and fitness class in Leicester and quickly learned to salsacise and do aerobics to speed up their progress. The overwhelming comment from them was that they didn't feel hungry and, considering the two guys were strapping six-footers, I was very pleasantly surprised.

Although scientific studies have shown that eating foods with a low glycaemic index can help prevent certain health problems, no clinical trials have proved that a low-Gi diet on its own helps you to lose weight. That's not really surprising because we have known for a very long time that to lose weight we need to eat fewer calories than we actually use up each day. We also know that eating low-fat foods is an easy way to cut back on the calories as, compared with carbohydrates or proteins, gram for gram, fat contains twice as many calories. And, if we add into the mix some regular moderate exercise, we can speed up the weight-loss process as well as further improving our overall health and fitness.

The key to an effective diet is simple. A diet needs to be easy to follow, enjoyable to eat, and not leave you feeling hungry. It should allow you some freedom to make your own choices whether at home or out socially, and have fast results that you can actually see and feel. There's nothing like initial success to inspire you on to greater success, so if you can see results on a diet, you are much more likely to stick with it. My aim is to take you on an enjoyable adventure towards the body you have always dreamed of. AND, YES, IT CAN BE DONE!

A quick guide to Gi

Gi stands for glycaemic index, which measures the speed at which carbohydrate foods are digested and absorbed into the bloodstream. Foods with a low Gi rating are slowly absorbed and cause our blood sugar (glucose) to rise gently and then fall gradually. On the other hand, foods with a high Gi rating cause a rapid but short-term surge in our blood-sugar levels, which later drop suddenly and results in real hunger cravings, leading to snack-attacks for more quick-fix, high-Gi-rated foods.

The glycaemic index was originally created with the specific purpose of helping diabetics control their insulin levels. Studies involving the use of low-Gi foods have shown that a low-Gi diet can also play a very important role in the prevention of heart disease and significantly reduce the risk of developing diabetes.

This is a weight-loss book, so you will not find detailed tables listing the Gi values of foods here, because you simply don't need them. It is also important to realise that NOT EVERY food you eat needs to be low Gi. The aim is to eat a healthy diet that contains a higher proportion of foods with a low Gi rating than perhaps you used to eat.

Why Gi Jeans?

Why did I call it the Gi Jeans Diet? Because I know how I feel when I look good in my jeans – I feel top dollar! I am very conscious of what I eat, so my weight only fluctuates by a few pounds from time to time, but my jeans are my barometer of how I'm doing on the weight front. Virtually everyone – both men and women – likes to look great in jeans, with no stomach overhanging. And almost every overweight person I have ever met wants to look good in jeans as an incentive to stick with their diet programme. Jeans are unforgiving, so we know that if we look and feel good in them, then we feel more confident about our bodies and ourselves generally. If you can trim your body so that you look great in yours, you will have every incentive to keep eating healthily, working out regularly and enjoying life in the long term, and THAT is what we are after!

About the Gi Jeans Diet

My Gi Jeans Diet includes two eating plans. The main Gi Jeans Diet is the most effective and will give the fastest results. However, for those people who hate sticking to a diet plan, I have created the No Diet Gi Jeans Diet plan, which gives you more freedom, although there are still guidelines on which foods you can and can't eat! You will also find lots of easy-to-prepare, delicious recipes, the most effective body toning exercises ever (to help improve your shape while you slim) and fat-burning aerobic exercise suggestions to help you burn your body fat faster. And, if you are not keen on exercising, I've included a quiz to enable you to find out which type of exercise is best suited to your personality so that you will have a greater chance of success. In between all this there is bags of motivation and information so that you can make informed choices about your lifestyle in the future.

GI AT A GLANCE

- Gi (glycaemic index) rates carbohydrate foods on the speed at which they are digested and absorbed into the bloodstream.
- Foods with a low Gi rating are slowly absorbed and our blood sugar levels rise gently and then fall gradually, which helps us feel fuller for longer and less inclined to snack.
- Foods with a high Gi rating lead to a rapid surge in blood sugar levels, which later drop suddenly, leading to hunger cravings for more quick-fix foods.
- Studies have shown that a low-Gi diet can help prevent heart disease and significantly reduce the risk of developing diabetes.

2 A crash course in Gi and GL

When we talk about the glycaemic index we are talking about carbohydrates – that's foods such as bread, rice, pasta, cereal and potatoes, although carbohydrate is also found in all fruits and vegetables and some other foods.

We have always been led to believe that 'simple' carbohydrates, such as refined sugars and sweets, are bad and that 'complex' carbohydrates, such as bread, cereal, pasta, rice and potatoes, are good. The rationale behind this theory was that 'simple' carbohydrates are rapidly absorbed into the bloodstream whereas starchy carbohydrates such as potatoes, rice and pasta are more slowly digested. In reality, it is not as simple as that. The rate at which the energy from carbohydrate enters the bloodstream depends on many different factors, including the exact type of starch and the method of cooking.

The glycaemic index is a way of ranking foods based on the rate at which they raise our blood sugar (glucose) levels. Each food is given a rating on a scale of 1-100, and the lower the rating, the better. Glucose is the highest-ranking food at 100 and other carbohydrates are gauged somewhere in between. Generally speaking, anything with a rating of 70 or over is considered 'high' Gi, a rating between 69 to 55 can be considered 'medium', and under 55 is considered 'low'. However, you can 'shift' the Gi value by combining different foods. Most of the foods included in my Gi Jeans Diet eating plan are low Gi, but occasionally I have combined 'high' Gi foods with 'low' Gi ones to make a 'medium' Gi meal which is still healthy and most likely an improvement on what you used to eat prior to following this plan.

Keeping our blood glucose levels stable can improve our sensitivity to a hormone we all have in our body called insulin. It was for this reason that the glycaemic index was originally created, as diabetics struggle to keep their insulin levels balanced. Failure to do so can result in serious consequences for them.

People who are overweight can be less sensitive to insulin, compared to people who are a healthy weight. This makes them more prone to diabetes, and it can also lead to heart problems. It makes sense, therefore, to take preventative action to avoid serious health risks, and we can do this easily by incorporating low-Gi foods into our daily diet and losing those unwanted pounds to achieve a healthier weight.

Low-Gi diets are based around fibre-rich foods and include lots of fresh fruit and vegetables and generous helpings of legumes (beans and pulses). Fibre is a crucial component of any healthy Gi diet, and in many cases, the higher the fibre content, the lower the Gi ranking is likely to be. So when you are shopping check the labels and always opt for the higher-fibre alternatives. However, be aware that some low-Gi foods can be quite high in fat, so only select foods with 5% or less fat content.

Gi and weight loss

A low-Gi diet will only help weight loss if it helps to cut calories. Low-Gi foods such as beans and pulses, vegetables and fruit are naturally low in calories. In addition, the high fibre content of many low-Gi foods helps to keep us feeling fuller for longer as the stomach doesn't empty as fast as it does after eating very highly processed foods. Since a diet based on low-Gi foods reduces dramatic fluctuations in blood glucose and insulin levels, it decreases hunger pangs – a real bonus when trying to lose weight. Also, by eating foods which have a low Gi rating, you will automatically be giving many high-fat, high-calorie foods such as cakes, biscuits, confectionery and high-sugar soft drinks a miss, which will, of course, speed up your weight-loss progress.

There is no EU law or legal definition of low Gi and, technically, it is not a nutrition claim for a product. Currently a Gi claim on a product needs to be substantiated by a controlled feeding trial to measure the release of sugar into the blood compared to glucose. There are numerous factors that affect the glycaemic index, so usually a high, medium or low system, rather than a specific number, is used by manufacturers and retailers, such as Tesco, who are the leaders in this field.

Since the fat content can lower the Gi rating of foods, don't fall into the high-fat trap. Remember, fat makes you fat! The purpose of this book is to help you lose weight. The most effective way to lose weight is to follow a low-fat, calorie-controlled diet and that is the difference between the diet in this book and many other Gi diets that have been published. So, you need to choose low-fat foods, then select low-Gi ones, too. Make sure that you only select products with 5% or less fat, i.e. 5 grams or less per 100 grams of product, unless otherwise stated in the diet plan. Providing you follow that guideline and keep within the calorie allowance given for that meal, you will be able to substitute your own choices for some of the Gi Jeans Diet meal suggestions.

General Gi guidelines

BEANS AND PULSES are naturally high in fibre and offer slow-releasing energy, which makes them ideal low-Gi foods. Adding them to casseroles and soups can reduce the Gi rating of the dish.

BREAD varies enormously in its Gi rating. These days you can find a wide variety of grains made into bread. As a rule of thumb, the critical factor is the fibre content, so ideally choose seedy loaves made from stone-ground flour rather than plain bread. When it comes to labelling statements, avoid those with descriptions such as 'unbleached' or 'enriched' flour, which is actually white flour when all the nutrients from the wheatgerm and bread have been stripped away but a few minerals and vitamins have been added back. Whenever possible, choose bread where the flour has been stoneground, as it will be coarser, or loaves with seeds and grains still intact. Some loaves are now being produced with added ingredients such as beta-glucan (usually found in oats) to lower the Gi. These breads tend to be more expensive but may be worth investing in if you eat a lot of bread. Pitta bread and tortilla wraps have a lower Gi than ordinary loaves and so are good choices, too, and make great sandwich alternatives for a quick lunch.

CEREAL is another minefield but the frontrunner here without a doubt is oats and the coarser the flakes the better. While oats are around 8% fat, they are packed with essential nutrients and are usually cooked or served with water or milk, which brings down the overall fat content. Instant porridge oats are also good – make them up with water and serve with semi-skimmed milk and a little sugar or honey for a long-lasting, energy-giving break-fast. Wholegrain muesli that has not been overly processed is a good choice, too, as is any high-fibre cereal such as All-Bran, Bran Buds and Shredded Wheat. Special K is also a low-Gi food. Weetabix is borderline medium Gi but is included in this eating plan because of its natural nutritional qualities.

A QUICK GUIDE TO LOW GI

- Choose whole-oat cereals for breakfast rather than refined corn or rice ones.
- Select multigrain or stoneground bread or loaves containing intact seeds and grains in place of ordinary white or brown bread.
- Pitta bread and tortilla wraps make great sandwich alternatives.
- Waxy new potatoes have a lower Gi than old potatoes.
- Pasta has a lower Gi than potatoes or rice.
- Basmati rice has a lower Gi than other varieties of rice. Avoid easy-cook brands.
- Add beans and pulses to stews and casseroles, and salads and soups to reduce the overall Gi content of your meal.
- Use low-calorie, low-Gi fillers such as tomatoes, beansprouts, chopped celery and courgettes to 'bulk up' meals and give you more chewing power.
- Eat fruit in place of cakes and biscuits.
- Avoid over-ripe bananas – they have a higher Gi rating than less ripe ones.
- Drink water in place of high-sugar drinks.

PASTA has a lower Gi than bread, potatoes or rice and so is a great food to include in a low-Gi diet.

POTATOES vary quite dramatically in their Gi ranking. Sweet potatoes have the lowest Gi rating. New potatoes, with their waxy texture, are also a good choice, whereas old potatoes are a high-Gi food. However, if you cook a jacket potato ('high' Gi) in the oven and then serve it with baked beans ('low' Gi), it becomes a 'medium' Gi meal, which is fine and healthy. Always cook potatoes in their skins for increased fibre.

RICE varies enormously in its Gi content. Basmati rice has a much lower Gi than regular varieties. Easy-cook rice has a particularly high Gi, so it's worth taking a few more minutes to prepare the traditional varieties.

What about glycaemic load?

A recent progression of the glycaemic index has been the discovery of glycaemic load (GL). This is a calculation of the Gi value and carbohydrate content per serving of food. It takes into account the amount of carbohydrate in the meal and the type of carbohydrate (its Gi value). Both are equally important and they both have an effect on blood sugar levels. Researchers at Harvard University in the USA came up with a way of combining these two factors and called it the 'glycaemic load'.

Calculating the GL values of food is particularly beneficial for diabetics, but it should not be used on its own as a weight-loss tool as the likelihood is that the dieter will not eat a balanced diet, which would be counter-productive. However, by incorporating low-Gi foods into your diet you will automatically reduce the glycaemic load.

This is a weight-loss diet book designed to give you the optimum healthy diet to achieve a dramatic weight loss. There are many other books on the market outlining specific Gi and GL values of foods if this is of particular interest to you. What is different about this Gi Jeans Diet book is that the diet has already been tested by real dieters – with amazing weight-loss results – without resorting to counting every Gi point.

3 So you want to lose weight?

You've made the decision to lose weight. Now it's time to put it into practice. Take it one step at a time – start by focusing on the benefits you will reap – and you will definitely achieve your goal.

It may be the first time you have tried to lose weight or it may be that you have been trying to lose weight for a while. Nevertheless, look upon today as the day you start your diet. It's good to see each day as a unit. If it turns out to be a good diet-day you can feel proud of yourself. If it becomes a disaster diet-day, just 'turn the page' in your mind and start afresh tomorrow.

You will achieve your new slim figure over time – it's a 'work in progress', but it is the best 'work' you will ever do. Why? Because achieving a healthy weight will make a major contribution to your achieving a healthier body.

You may want to lose weight to make you look and feel better but you should never underestimate the dramatic effect it will have on your health. We keep telling ourselves that heart disease and diabetes are conditions that affect other people. They're not. They can affect all of us and it's important to take action NOW to reverse any damage done so far. The good news is that your body will respond very quickly to the positive changes the diet in this book will help you to make.

More and more scientific research shows that obesity is a major cause of Type 2 diabetes, heart disease, some cancers and high blood pressure. These are serious life-threatening conditions, yet it is totally within your control to turn your risk of suffering them around. All you have to do is make some small lifestyle changes. If you were to eat less fat and fewer processed foods, give yourself smaller portions and become generally more active, you could dramatically reduce your chances of suffering a premature death.

Find a reason to lose weight

When I ask successful slimmers what made them stop gaining weight and start losing it, I receive the same answers I've heard so many times before. 'I didn't want to be the "fat mum" at the school gates.' 'My doctor told me I would die early if I didn't lose weight.' 'I saw a photograph of myself at my niece's wedding and I couldn't believe that great fat person was actually me,' and the all-time favourite: 'I saw myself on video.' The problem is that lots of overweight people are in denial about how big they are.

Many overweight people don't even possess a mirror that shows below shoulder height. They buy clothes with elastic waistbands so that they don't know what their size really is. They often wear the same few clothes that fit, for months, not daring to go into a dress shop to buy new ones in case the size is bigger than last time. Being overweight, or dare I say obese, is like having a great big cloud affecting every minute of every day and indeed everything in your life – how people treat you, how fast you can move about, the pain you feel in your knees when you climb the stairs and, of course, the feeling of permanent exhaustion.

The word 'obese' is an ugly word that brings with it con-notations of greed, lack of self-respect and laziness. Change those unkind words to 'love of food', 'lack of confidence' and 'inactive' and you realise it describes a totally normal person who has 'let things get a little out of control.' It happens. Many people have a part of their life that is out of control. It may be debt, addiction, infidelity – who knows? But the fact is that if you are seriously overweight or obese it's OK! You are not ready to be 'certified' but you are a good and worthy member of society who has the CHOICE to change your body size and become healthier.

How we lose weight

With so many different types of diet around, it's not surprising that people get confused. You may have followed endless diets and even enjoyed some success but it is really important to understand the basic facts of how a diet works if you are going to lose weight satisfactorily.

The human body needs food to give it energy to function, in the same way that a central heating system needs fuel in the form of gas, electricity, oil, or solid fuel. Whereas a central heating system is designed to accept as much fuel as it needs, when it needs it, we have to rely on meal times and snacks to give our bodies a regular supply of fuel. The problem comes when our ordering system is out of sync with our bodily needs. This results in an over-delivery of food, which then has to be stored – as fat. That's when we gain weight. It is the same as having excess deliveries of fuel for your central heating system and having to build extra coal bunkers or oil tanks in which to store it. Fat is stored in fat cells all around the body and when each fat cell is filled to capacity, we automatically create more, but *we* are in control of how full or empty they are.

To lose weight you need to adjust your 'goods inwards' deliveries so that you receive fewer food calories than you actually burn each day and start using up some of your existing fat stores to make up the difference.

Metabolism

Every day the body spends around 2000 calories (around 3000 for men) to make it function and to enable you to be physically active – in other words, just 'living'. You can't stop yourself from using that fuel (although you would burn around 600 fewer calories if you stayed in bed all day). Unless you are ill, you are unlikely to be in bed all day – you will be out and about, living your daily life. The body HAS to get those calories from somewhere. If they don't come from food (because you are on a calorie-reduced diet), your body will automatically make up the difference by calling on the calories stored around your body as fat. This will lead to weight loss and inch reduction. It's a simple matter of physics. For any diet to enable you to lose weight, it HAS to feed you fewer calories than your body actually burns up.

You should never follow a diet of fewer than 1200 calories for more than two weeks as this would result in your body holding on to your fat to protect you against future starvation. You would then lose muscle instead of fat, which is the very last thing you want. This is why crash diets don't work, because if you follow them for longer than two weeks your body's metabolic rate could slow down to conserve energy.

Muscle is energy-hungry tissue and needs calories to sustain it, whereas fat requires very little energy. So, if you give your body sufficient calories to meet its basic needs (around 1400 –1500 calories a day for women and 1700–1800 for men, depending on your age and current weight), your body will not think it is starving and will tick over very happily.

However, by reducing your food intake by a further 200 or 300 calories, down to 1200 calories, for just a couple of weeks, which is what my Gi Jeans Kick-start Diet does, you will see a dramatic fall in weight as, in effect, you take the body by surprise. But if you were to continue on the lower calorie level after two weeks your rate of weight loss would slow down considerably. That is why, after week two, I have given you a more generous calorie allowance. The interesting thing is that your overall progress will ultimately be faster by eating more, as in Part 2 of the Gi Jeans Diet, because your body will not feel under threat of starvation and will happily burn up its fat stores to meet its energy needs. This doesn't mean to say that you can't reintroduce the Gi Jeans Kick-start Diet again for a week or two every couple of months if you can cope with it. If you can, your rate of progress will be amazing, but it's important that you do not stay on it for longer than two weeks at a time.

So, a daily calorie allowance of around 1400 or 1500 would sustain your basal metabolic rate (BMR) but cause your energy supply to fall short of its needs by about 600 calories a day. As those calories have to be found from somewhere, 600 calories-worth of body fat gets burned away as emergency fuel to make up the difference. Brilliant! And here's the clever bit. If you eat your 1400 or 1500 calories in the form of food that is low Gi and low in fat, you shouldn't FEEL that you are eating less quantity of food than you did before.

Once you have completed the Gi Jeans Kick-start Diet, turn to the BMR (Basal Metabolic Rate) charts on pages 312–315.

These illustrate your personal calorie allowance, based on your age, gender and current weight. This will enable you to eat sufficient calories to meet your bodily needs yet few enough to affect a weight loss. With this information at your fingertips you can be sure you will be maximising your potential success. As you lose weight you will be able to adjust your calorie allowance to ensure that your rate of weight loss is maintained.

Why low fat?

Fat in food doesn't make the food 'bigger' or more filling, so it doesn't affect the quantity of food you want to eat. Compared to carbohydrate or protein, fat contains twice as many calories, so reducing your fat intake is an obvious target when trying to cut calories.

Carbohydrates give us energy (like fuel in a car) and are burned as fuel very easily. Protein is utilised by the body for growth and repair of muscles, organs, tissue, and so on, and is also not easily laid down as fat. Conversely, the fat that we eat is very easily stored as body fat and is processed by the body quite differently. Nature designed us to be fat-storers because food has not always been available 24/7. There were, and still are in some countries, times of famine, so our bodies are designed to protect us in case we are unable to get food.

Let me explain this a little further. Carbohydrate is digested in the stomach and goes to the small intestine and then into the bloodstream for cellular use as energy. It is stored in the muscles for use when we need it and for energy when we exercise. If we eat too much, however, it will be stored as fat.

Protein is digested in a similar way. When it reaches the bloodstream it gets used for repair of cells around the body.

Again, though, if we eat too much protein, it will be stored as fat.

Fat is digested differently. It goes to the stomach, where it forms clusters of fat. Because it is lumpy, it cannot enter the bloodstream like carbohydrate or protein but instead goes into the lymphatic system. It is then transported around the body, after which the clusters are broken down and the fat in our blood rises. Fat can stick to our blood vessels, which is why our cholesterol can rise and cause heart problems. Only a very small amount of fat – about 10 per cent – is taken up by the muscles as energy and the remaining 90 per cent will be transported around the body to be stored, making us fatter. However, if we exercise regularly, our bodies become much more efficient in burning fat as energy.

It is obvious, then, that fat really is the enemy when we are trying to lose weight. By cutting right down on our fat intake we can reduce the calories AND avoid adding to our existing fat stores, with significant benefits to our health.

If we combine low-fat eating with eating healthy low-Gi foods, with their slow-releasing energy qualities that stave off hunger pangs, we have the recipe for the perfect weight-loss diet. It really is a win–win situation.

I cannot complete this discussion about fat without mentioning saturated and poly- or mono-unsaturated fats. ALL fats have a similar fattening power, so if you are trying to lose weight, cut back on them all. Be aware that olive oil – or any oil for that matter – is 100 per cent fat! However, if you are slim and at risk of developing heart disease, then mono- or poly-unsaturated fats are fine. The only exception is that everyone should eat one portion of oily fish each week to ensure a regular intake of important omega-3 fish oils.

So let's take some simple steps to a new you. Here are five golden rules.

1 Eat three meals a day, including breakfast, plus two Power Snacks and one Treat (see pages 91–2).

2 Eat a higher proportion of natural foods and reduce your intake of highly processed foods to give your overall diet a lower Gi rating. Eat plenty of fresh fruit and vegetables and try to avoid highly processed, high-sugar, high-fat snacks.

3 Eat foods with 5% or less fat, with the exception of oily fish, e.g. salmon or mackerel, once a week and some brands of multigrain bread.

4 Drink lots of water and drink alcohol only in moderation.

5 Start being more active *every* day. Remember you burn twice as many calories standing rather than sitting, walking rather than standing, and jogging rather than walking!

Make these five golden rules part of your everyday life and you'll change your body for ever.

4 How to be a weight-loss winner

If you want to lose weight safely and effectively, as well as understanding the principles of a healthy diet and what types of food to eat, you need to get your mind into gear and adopt some simple strategies that will help motivate you and enable you to achieve ultimate slimming success.

Set some goals

We all need goals to motivate us into action but unless we make those goals more specific, we may never achieve them. We all need a reason for making that extra bit of effort or to try that bit harder. With goals to aim for, we will achieve so much more than if we have nothing to focus on.

If you want to lose weight you need to imagine the huge benefits you will enjoy and you need to say them to yourself in the first person, e.g. I will have more energy, I will look more attractive, my clothes will fit better, my joints won't ache, my health will improve, my self-confidence will increase and I will receive compliments about how good I look and recognition for what I have achieved. Wow!

The good news is that these goals ARE DEFINITELY ACHIEV-ABLE! It is down to that initial decision – 'I am going to lose weight' – and then the preparation to commence. It does take a bit of planning – making some changes to your shopping list, how you cook your food and what you do with your leisure time. Sitting and watching television for 27 hours a week is not an option if you want to see real results and quickly. I know that if I sat for almost four hours every day I would gain weight. I need to stay active if I am to stay trim and eat the quantity of food I want.

Goal-setting sounds easy – 'I want to lose 2st for my summer holiday and I want to get fit' – but it isn't as simple as that. How are you actually going to achieve this goal? Perhaps you fancy taking up jogging or joining a fitness class? These are things that will help, but what are YOU going to do YOURSELF? You need to be very specific and you need to make a plan.

Your overall goal may be to lose 2st in time for your summer holiday, but what does that actually mean? If your holiday is, say, 21 weeks away it means that you will need to lose about 1½lb per week between now and then. That is very achievable and very measurable. So write down on your Goal Sheet: 'Lose 1½lb a week'.

How will you achieve this? You will need to follow a diet. How is this going to affect your normal way of life? Make a few pledges to yourself and write them down. It might go something like this:

'No more chocolate at work. Take chopped raw veg instead.'
'I will only drink on Friday, Saturday and Sunday evenings – max. 2 glasses of wine on each day.'

Now, what about exercise and activity? 'Well, I'll try and do 20–30 minutes of exercise on five days a week – that's right isn't it?' Yes, but WHEN will you exercise? Be more specific. Try this:

Monday – Go to RC Diet and Fitness Club class p.m.
Tuesday – Meet up with Sally and take dogs for extra long walk after work.
Wednesday – Mow the lawn p.m.
Thursday – Do toning workout to fitness video/DVD or do salsacise workout (e.g. Rosemary Conley DVD) before work.
Friday – Rest day.
Saturday – Do housework then take children for long walk and picnic if fine weather; swimming if not.
Sunday – Gardening plus 30 minutes of physical activity with family in the garden.

What about in the kitchen? What changes can you make to your food preparation? What about these?

'Stop using oil or fat when cooking.'
'Stop adding butter to the vegetables when I serve them or adding it to the mashed potatoes.'

You know where your danger zones are and, if you want to achieve a slim, attractive, healthy body, you will have to make some changes to the way you feed it and look after it. The rewards are so enormous. If you could feel those benefits today you wouldn't hesitate to start right now.

Get rid of your excuses

Some people know why they have gained weight. They acknowl-edge that they eat too many high-fat snacks and drink too much alcohol and do too little exercise or activity. Others are puzzled. They don't eat anything in excess and can't understand why they are now wearing a size 16 when it used to be a size 12. They don't binge, they are not greedy and they are active. It all seems so unfair. 'It must be my metabolism,' they say. Unfortunately it isn't.

Whether you know the reasons for your overweight or not, is only for you to ponder. One thing for sure – if you weigh more now than you did a year ago it is because you have taken in more calories in the form of food than you have spent in the form of exercise and activity.

Record your progress

It is a proven fact that writing down what you eat every day is one of the best ways to help you become more aware of your eating and snacking habits. When any of the members of my classes is struggling and has not lost weight in a particular week, the instructor will issue them with a Diet Record Sheet. Almost every time a member fills in a sheet, they lose more weight. Why?

I believe there are two reasons – firstly they have been given a task to fulfil and must make an extra effort if they don't want to let their instructor down. If they cheat, they not only have to admit it to the person who is trying to help them but also, more importantly, to themselves. Writing it down helps them to recog-nise where they might be going wrong and why they are not losing weight.

The second benefit is the designated time period – one week during which they must write down their food and drink intake. One week isn't long, so it gives them an acceptable challenge and a real focus for that week. Writing down what you eat and drink will work for anyone, so give it a try and see the results.

To help slimmers I have produced a Gi Jeans Diet Journal which enables you to keep a diary record of all that you eat and drink, your exercise and other activity achieved as well as motivational advice to keep you going (see back of book for further details).

Find a support group

Research has shown that dieting with others is more effective than dieting on your own and that's why members of my Diet and Fitness Clubs are so successful. Not only are they weighed on professional scales every week, they also receive advice and a workout designed for people of all ages and abilities. All of the instructors are professionally qualified to teach exercise to music and are also qualified in nutrition and will give you sound advice suited to your specific needs. They are very special people who want to help others to lose weight safely and effectively and have fun along the way.

If there's no class near you, try my Postal Slimming Pack (www.rosemary-conley.co.uk) or my online slimming club at www.slimwithRosemary.com. All of these methods of weight loss are proven to work, are extremely popular and all of them include this Gi Jeans Diet programme.

Speed up your weight loss

If you want to lose weight fast and effectively, healthily and have a good-looking body shape at the end of it, you must introduce exercise into your lifestyle. Don't worry, you can find something that you will enjoy doing and my Fitness Quiz (see pages 251–3) will help you to find out which type of exercise will suit you best. An easy way to motivate yourself to be more active is to wear a pedometer and aim to do 10,000 steps a day.

Exercise burns EXTRA calories and works the heart and lungs to make us fitter and healthier. Exercise also turns our muscles into calorie-burning-engines and makes the body a more efficient 'fat-burner'. And we don't just reap the benefits during our exercise session as it causes us to burn more calories even when we have stopped exercising. Exercise also helps our skin to shrink as we slim, it tones up our bodies and gives us a better shape. Exercise can also reduce our risk of having a heart attack or stroke, lower our blood pressure, help us to sleep, cope better with stress, be more alert . . . . Need I go on?

Exercise regularly and you will not only speed up your rate of weight loss dramatically, but you will also find it much easier to maintain your new weight in the long term.

The common excuse for not exercising is that we don't have time. It's not that we don't have really good intentions. We do. It's just that we will only do it after all the other 'things' in our life are done. And, of course, they never are, so exercise gets missed. So make a plan. Exercise is VERY important. It deserves to go near the top of your list!

TEN WAYS TO LOSE WEIGHT FASTER

1 Make a plan for your exercise sessions and stick to it.
2 Write down everything you eat and drink.
3 Write the items down as you consume them, not at the end of the day.
4 Invite someone to exercise with you – it will make you more committed and it will be more fun.
5 If you go to an exercise class, think about going to an extra one on another day.
6 Try different forms of exercise such as dancing or a sport.
7 Build into your week some activity that you can do as a family or with friends such as all going swimming or for a cycle ride.
8 Try to do some exercise each week early in the day. If you can manage it, an early morning walk or jog is a great way to wake up your body and make you feel on top form for the rest of the day. You will also find your willpower is so much stronger that day because you won't want to 'waste' the physical effort that you put in earlier by snacking unnecessarily later on.
9 Exercise releases happy hormones called endorphins, so not only will you experience physical benefits but you will feel better mentally, too. You will find you can concentrate better as well as cope more easily with whatever the day throws at you.
10 Always remember to think positively and you are more likely to see positive results. Remember, it is up to you and only you. As it says in the Nike advertisement – 'Just do it!'

5 Change your attitude towards food

Do you think about food all the time? Do you worry about your obsession with food? Well, the good news is that you can retrain your brain. I know, I've done it!

When I was in my twenties I was obsessed about food and my weight. I had gained almost 2½st as a result of falling in love with food after doing a Cordon Bleu cookery course. At 5ft 2in tall, small boned and weighing 10st 4lb, I looked significantly overweight. The food I cooked was so delicious I just couldn't stop eating it! And the harder I tried to lose weight, the more it seemed to go on.

I can remember standing in front of the mirror in the bedroom at home, on the brink of tears, despairing at what to wear because I had gained so much weight and nothing in my wardrobe fitted. I can remember saying 'you big fat cow' out loud to myself and then promising myself that this was it. I was not going to buy the next dress size up – a size 16. I was going to go on a diet and lose weight. Definitely! Now!

Then I went downstairs and, without realising what I was doing, I toasted a round of bread, spread it thickly with butter and topped it with lots of marmalade – and ate it. Then another slice. And then another! At this point I remember coming to my senses and realising what I had done. I was beside myself. I honestly felt I was going mad. The frightening thing was that this uncontrollable bingeing happened quite regularly.

Well, that was more than 30 years ago, but I can remember the feelings of panic as if it were yesterday. I struggled to lose my excess 2½st over the following months and battled to keep my weight down for many years thereafter. It was because of those feelings that I started my own slimming classes to help others who loved food just as much as I did and who wanted to be slim more than anything in the world yet, like me, just carried on sabotaging their attempts.

So, how did I change my thought processes to give me the healthy attitude to food that I have today? I don't binge any more. I know what it's like to feel full. I can put my knife and fork down and leave food on the side of my plate without feeling guilty about the starving millions. I can throw leftovers away and not feel bad about it. For someone who has not been a serial dieter, that sounds unimportant. If you are a 'foodie', you will appreciate just how monumental this transformation was and you will want to get there too. This is how I cracked it – just follow these simple tips and there's no reason why you shouldn't crack it, too.

Don't keep weighing yourself

If you go to a class, weigh yourself there rather than at home. Weighing yourself every day – some people even weigh themselves several times a day – is madness. It is misleading, unrealistic and really unhelpful.

Plan ahead

Plan your week's meals and then prepare your shopping list. If you don't, you will be thinking all day 'what shall we have tonight?' and food will be too much on your mind. If you know what you will be having, and you have the ingredients, you don't have to think about it at all until you start cooking.

Select foods you enjoy

Select foods you enjoy and that also fill you up at all three meal-times. My Gi Jeans Diet includes a variety of foods designed to fill you up, and you should easily find ones that suit your taste. Some people may have a preference for a particular breakfast cereal – because they like the taste, or they want one with a high-fibre content to keep them regular or a high-bulk/low-calorie one to give them a bigger bowlful. Choose what you want, but select one that will keep you going until lunchtime and remember that high-fibre, low-Gi ones will do that best of all.

Recognise your trigger foods

These are the foods that once you have a taste of them you can't stop eating them. For me this is definitely Pringles! I 'manage' this by only buying a mini pack very occasionally, for instance on holiday, and then sharing them with my husband, Mike. You can still have such foods but they must be seen as an allowable, occasional treat, not a forbidden food that you binge on only because you know you shouldn't be eating it!

Fill up on vegetables

If you have a large appetite, then fill up on low-fat, low-calorie vegetables with a low-Gi rating. Pile them high alongside your meat, fish or chicken and enjoy them. Also, tomatoes, grated carrots, beansprouts, celery and courgettes can all be used to 'bulk-up' recipes to give you more chewing power, larger portions and great taste as well as lots of extra nutrients.

Don't panic if you can't choose your food

Sometimes we get invited out and find ourselves presented with food that is wonderful but not low fat or low Gi. Don't worry! Eat it and enjoy it BUT have just a moderate portion and don't have second helpings. Be more active the next day and get back on track. You don't have to be a diet bore, just be sensible.

Fill up with a long drink before each meal

Drink a large glass of water before each meal. This will help you to feel fuller quicker and aid your weight-loss or weight-maintenance progress. Having a long drink before you start eating can take the edge off your appetite and stop you overeating too quickly because you are hungry. It takes time for food to reach your stomach and for your brain to register that you have had enough. A drink will reach your stomach quicker than food and then it will be ready to swell out the food that you eat to give you a fuller feeling. If, like me, you are not a huge water fan, drink flavoured varieties or opt for low-calorie drinks.

Train your brain not to think about food

You are in control of your brain and you can train it to change its thought patterns. If you find yourself thinking about buying a chocolate bar, just tell your brain you can't do that (just as you can tell your brain that you can't rob that bank or steal that car), then consciously think about something else. You could phone a friend or go for a walk or do an odd job. Whatever it is, just don't allow your brain to ponder on the temptation of the moment that you know will sabotage your weight-loss efforts.

Realise that food is your friend, not your enemy

If you didn't eat food you would die. If you regularly ate too much of the wrong kinds of food, it could lead to serious, life-threatening, illnesses. On the other hand, eating sensible portions of the right foods can provide you with an amazing energy and zest for life beyond your three score years and ten! You'll then have a healthy body that will enable you to live a long and active life and achieve so much. I wonder why we put so little importance on the nutritional value of the food we eat when it can make us feel so good when we get it right. So make sure you give yourself five-star fuel.

Keeping portions in proportion

Portion sizes in restaurants are getting bigger, offering better value for money, but unless we learn portion control we will never reach our weight-loss goals.

We've all seen banners like this: 'SUNDAY LUNCH BUFFET, EAT AS MUCH AS YOU LIKE FOR £7.99!' A fast food chain offers three bumper burgers for the price of two. Your favourite chocolate bar is on offer at '30% extra FREE'. It's not surprising we are struggling to fight obesity when the salesmen are tempting us to buy their products because you get more for your money.

We know we become overweight because we eat too much food. We can all come up with 101 excuses why we don't have time to work out every day. Exercise definitely helps, but let's face it – it's what we put into our mouths that is the main culprit. 'But I don't overeat!' I hear you plea. Maybe you don't call into the newsagents each day and buy three bars of chocolate and four packets of crisps and devour them before lunchtime. But when it comes to dining out or just eating at home, your plate is piled high. 'But I'm hungry!' you cry. I am sure you are but you can TRAIN your appetite just as you can train your body to be fitter. And it needn't be as tough as you think.

Cut the calories but not the quantity

Compared with vegetables, meat and poultry are higher in calories, so just cut back on your portion of meat, perhaps by slicing it more thinly or just giving yourself one less slice, but increase your portion of your favourite veg. So, if you were to have 75g (3oz) roast beef instead of 150g (5oz) you would save 190 calories. Add 20 calories for an extra 50g (2oz) portion of both carrots and broccoli and 50 calories for an extra 50g (2oz) portion of new potatoes, and you would have a net saving of 120 calories without eating less food. One of the big messages given on any Gi diet is to try and fill half your plate with vegetables, a quarter with a serving of protein food such as meat, fish or poultry, and the remaining quarter with carbohydrate such as potatoes, rice or pasta. Always try and picture this image when placing food on your plate.

You don't have to have a huge portion in restaurants

If, like me, you enjoy selecting a three-course meal when dining out, consider pacing yourself and your calories by ordering your main course as a small portion. Some restaurants are happy to serve a starter-size main course and this can cut the calories by half (as well as the cost!), leaving you space and calories for a dessert. Fill up with low-calorie, high-nutrition green vegetables or salad with your main course and eat slowly to allow time for the food to reach your stomach. Wait between courses. Eat until you are full but not overfull and bloated.

It is not good for our long-term weight control to physically overstretch our stomachs. After all, we want to train them to shrink a bit, not stretch! That way we will automatically know when we have eaten enough and know when to stop. I never, ever thought I would be saying that, but honestly, it can be done. I have done it and it makes life SO much easier. I don't have to 'diet' now because my stomach tells me when to stop. Having been a habitual binge-eater for years I have to admit this is something of a miracle!

You don't have to eat everything!

We become overweight because we have eaten too much over a long period. We have been conditioned over generations that leaving food is sinful. It isn't. I know we rightly feel guilty about those who are starving and if we could send our leftovers to Africa we would, but we can't and there is absolutely no point in over-eating just to avoid waste. For years I wouldn't have dreamed of leaving food on my plate, but now I don't hesitate and I don't feel guilty about it. It may only be a bit of rice or pasta which I don't 'need' because I feel full enough – not over-full and uncomfortable. Learning this has turned around my ability to control my own weight, which I used to find so difficult and demoralising.

Weigh out your portions

Because we lead busy lives we naturally go for the quick option. We pour out our breakfast cereal and guess what an ounce or two looks like. We buy different types of loaves of bread, but do we check the nutrition panel to find out the number of calories per slice? They vary a lot! Do we weigh out our portion of meat and vegetables when serving up for the whole family? What about our serving of rice or pasta? These are all danger areas where 'just a little bit extra' could be sabotaging your weight-loss progress. Learn to cook fewer potatoes so that there aren't any or as many left over. Select a slightly smaller steak or chicken breast for yourself.

Try using a handy measure, such as a tablespoon or cup. Once you have weighed out your food and worked out the portion size it contains, this can work well. Serious portion-watchers could consider purchasing my 'Nutriscales'. These not only weigh the food but also calculate exactly how many calories, how much fat, cholesterol, carbohydrate and fibre is in it at the press of a button (for further information see www.rosemary-conley.co.uk).

Reduce your portion size by 20 per cent

Try putting one potato back or having one slice less of chicken or beef. When serving your dessert, use a smaller serving spoon but the same number of spoonfuls. If you have sugar on your cereal or in tea and coffee, cut it down by half a spoonful or try using a low-calorie alternative. When serving your pasta or rice, give yourself one spoonful less. All of these small reductions add up to a big drop in calories over a day and can make a real difference to your weight-loss progress.

When the going gets tough

No matter how hard we try and stick to the straight and narrow, there will be times when it all goes pear-shaped. That's life. Here's an excerpt from a letter I received from one of my dieters which sums up a typical experience:

'I was doing so well with my diet and I felt that this time was different,' wrote Susan. 'I've tried so many diets over the years but this time I felt really determined and I was losing steadily at the rate of 2lb a week. After losing a stone I could see and FEEL the difference. I felt really confident I would reach my goal this time and then we went away for a weekend break. The hotel was fabulous and the deal was all-inclusive. The food was out of this world and you could just help yourself from the buffet at every meal. I don't know what came over me but I just couldn't resist! I just ate and ate! Over three days I gained

7lb! I was mortified. Since I came home I seem to have lost the plot. Much as I try to get back on track I find myself thinking of chocolate, cream, biscuits and puddings all the time! I feel like I'm going mad! What has happened to me?'

We can probably all relate to Susan's situation. We seem to have to work so hard, consistently, to lose a mere 2lb a week yet we can pile it back on threefold, with very little effort, when we break all the low-fat rules. And THAT is the key. Even if you do eat significantly more food, if you can still eat foods that are low in fat the damage will be minimal. It's when you overindulge with the high-fat stuff that the pounds really pile on. Why? Because the fat that we eat is easily stored on our body as fat while carbohydrate and protein foods are easily burned off as energy.

We only draw on our fat stores for fuel when we are in energy (calorie) deficit. If we overeat, we will be in energy-surplus mode and the result is that the fat doesn't get burned off, it goes straight into storage – around our stomachs, hips, thighs, in fact anywhere that we easily fill out our fat cells and that depends on our individual body shape.

The other important factor to realise is that foods that are high in fat are also high in salt as, without the salty flavour, the foods wouldn't be palatable. Obviously the more salt we eat, the more fluid we retain and the body acts like a sponge. The consequence of this is that we weigh lots more on the scales – but be aware that it is 'artificially' more. No doubt Susan's eating extravaganza caused her to gain real fat – probably a couple of pounds – but the rest was almost certainly extra fluid retained by her body because of what she had eaten.

The facts are that for Susan to have gained 7lb of actual fat over her three days she would have had to have eaten 24,500 calories EXTRA in three days! With the best will in the world she could not have done that! This figure is calculated by multiplying one pound of fat, which equals 3,500 calories, by seven. Susan could have eaten around 2000 calories a day and her weight would have remained constant so she would have had to eat 10,000 calories a day for her three days to gain 7lb of fat!

So, what can we learn from this? First of all we need to realise that scales only tell us our overall weight status. While weighing ourselves weekly is extremely valuable in gauging our weight-loss progress, the reading does not take into account the different components making up that weight, e.g. fluid, fat, muscles, bone, etc. So don't become despondent if you know you have been sticking to your diet but nothing shows on the scales. You may well have lost inches.

Here are some tips to help you cope with tempting situations and to steer you back on track if you falter:

Watch out for eyes that are bigger than your stomach!

Research has shown that, after eating a large portion of the same food, we get bored and are happy to leave it. However, when we are confronted with lots of different tastes to tempt us, such as at a buffet, we can keep on going for much longer. Dangerous stuff when we are trying to shed those excess pounds!

Try to pick up a small plate and fill that rather than a huge one. I know it's not always easy to know what's what, but selecting high-fibre options of anything will help to keep the Gi content of your meal down.

Stick to low-fat choices

Even in the most lavish buffets there will always be some foods with less fat than others. Choose prawns, salmon and cold lean meats with some fresh wholegrain bread and a glass of wine and avoid anything deep-fried in breadcrumbs and pastries such as samosas, vol-au-vonts and sausage rolls. Pile your plate up with lots of oil-free salad garnish to fill you up and to nibble at as well as providing you with lots of low-Gi food. Give pork pie and cheese a wide berth as they are loaded with fat. Enjoy a dessert but go for something small and scrumptious rather than a huge slice of cheesecake or cream-laden gateau.

Appoint your own waiter!

If you know you can't be trusted at a buffet table, send your friend or partner to select your plate of food. Asking someone else to select for you means you don't get to see everything on offer and you won't know what you are missing.

Don't panic!

So you overindulged! It happens. Don't go near the scales for three days and get back on to your normal diet immediately. Also, get active! Go for a long walk. Work out to a fitness video. Do some gardening. If you immediately get back on track with sensible eating and increased activity you will be pleasantly surprised how quickly you will be back to normal.

Drink plenty of water

When we read that the body can hold on to fluid and that it can make us weigh heavier, it may discourage us from drinking water regularly. In fact the body is very efficient in eliminating fluids through the kidneys so we should drink water freely and it definitely will not affect our weight under normal circumstances. If we find ourselves feeling really thirsty, we must drink. If we don't we will become dehydrated which is harmful to health and detrimental to our appearance because it will affect our skin. If you have overindulged with fatty foods your body will soon regulate the fluid levels back to normal once you eat low-fat foods again, so don't worry.

So, make low-fat and low-Gi eating part of your everyday lifestyle. Don't worry if you do overdo it occasionally, we all do. Get back on track quickly and move on! Result? Long-term success.

6 Maximise your weight-loss success

If you want to lose weight faster and look your best along the way, you must get more active. Later in this book you will find some specific exercise programmes you may like to follow, but for now let's find out which sort of exercise does what.

With so many different types of exercise on offer it is easy to get confused. Different types of exercise deliver very different results, so it is crucial that you make informed choices when aiming to lose weight. The good news is that with the right type of exercise you can not only speed up your weight-loss progress, you can also IMPROVE YOUR BODY SHAPE and achieve a figure you probably never thought was possible!

So, what do you fancy? Aerobics or Pilates? Tai chi or yoga? Line dancing or Salsacise? Walking or jogging? Do they all help us to become slimmer and fitter? The answer is simple. No, they don't. They do very different things with a variety of results and benefits.

If you want to burn fat you need to do aerobic exercise

Any exercise or activity that causes you to breathe more deeply and automatically take in more oxygen is classed as 'aerobic'. Aerobic activities include walking, jogging, cycling, rowing, salsacise and, of course, aerobics classes and aqua-aerobics (aerobics in water).

Aerobic exercise does two very important jobs. It works the heart and lungs (that's why we get slightly breathless) which is great for general health and fitness, plus it causes us to actually burn fat from our bodies. That is the very best news for dieters!

When we do aerobic exercise we, in effect, 'turn up the gas' and we burn extra calories. This is obviously a tremendous help on a weight-reducing diet as it will speed up the process. Even more important is the fact that regular aerobic exercise causes the body to become a more efficient fat burner in everyday life – all the time. Imagine converting the engine in your car from a 1.6 litre to a 2.8 litre one – it will use more fuel! And the same thing happens to the body if we undertake regular aerobic exercise.

Everyone should do some kind of aerobic exercise on a regular basis. If you belong to a gym you will have access to a variety of cardiovascular equipment, including the treadmill, stepper, cross-trainer, exercise bike, rowing machine, etc. Group classes include step-aerobics, spinning, dancing, aerobics, line dancing and salsacise. Both spinning and salsacise burn more calories than most other types of aerobics do because they are faster. However, all of the above are brilliant fat-burners and it is just a matter of preference as to which one you choose. The most successful one for you will be the one you are happy to do regularly.

Pilates, tai chi, yoga and body-conditioning are not aerobic activities. They do various jobs, from developing our sense of balance, improving our flexibility, to toning the body. These activities are not fat burning, but they still fulfil an important function.

If you want to tone up your body, you need to do strength exercises

You've heard the saying 'use it or lose it'. Well this sums up our muscle strength. If we don't use our muscles regularly they will become smaller and weaker. As we get older our muscles will automatically reduce in size and over a period of ten years we could lose 10lb of muscle through wastage while naturally attracting more fat. We may weigh the same on the scales but that can change over time to reflect the added fat, plus our metabolic rate slows down. If you challenge your muscles regularly with strength exercises they will at least be sustained but hopefully will become larger and stronger. This doesn't mean we will end up looking like Arnold Schwarzenegger – far from it. Good muscle tone gives us a beautifully toned shape and good body strength to cope with everyday living.

Our muscles are made up of thousands of fibres. If we don't challenge these fibres in strength activities on a regular basis, some of the fibres become redundant and disappear over time. Conversely, if we regularly use those muscles in exercises where strength is the issue (e.g. by using weights at the gym or working with a strong resistance band) the muscle fibres increase in number to cope with the extra demand. Result: bigger muscles. This will not only give you a better shape but it will also increase your muscle mass. Muscle is energy-hungry tissue so the more muscle you have, the higher your metabolic rate. That's good news for those of us who enjoy food!

However, doing 100 sit-ups a day will not give you a flat stomach if you are overweight and have a fat stomach! Your hundred sit-ups may give you fabulously strong abdominal muscles but you won't see them because you have a layer of fat on top! To lose the fat from your stomach you need to do aerobic exercise as well as follow a low-fat, calorie-controlled diet.

Other 'strength' and 'toning' activities include Pilates, multi-gym, free weights, weight-lifting, as well as gentler but nevertheless very effective body-conditioning exercises. I have included my best-ever toning exercises in chapter 16 (and also in my *Shape Up & Salsacise* DVD). Practise these exercises regularly and you will see a dramatic difference in your shape.

Flexibility is vital to everyday life

Flexibility is incorporated in many forms of exercise. At the beginning and the end of your aerobics class you should stretch your muscles to help prevent injury during, and aching muscles later, but it also encourages greater flexibility of the joints and more elasticity of the muscles. Whether it is reaching up into a high cupboard, putting on our seat belt or zipping up the back of a dress, we need our bodies to be flexible.

Yoga is perhaps recognised as the most effective form of exercise to enhance flexibility as well as relaxation, although some of the postures could be considered controversial. Yoga is performed slowly and precisely with particular attention to breathing. With a greater understanding of anatomy and physiology in the 21st century, it's now thought that a few traditional yoga postures are best avoided by some individuals as they may over-extend certain joints, which could have a detrimental effect. Yoga will not make you lose weight but it can help to improve posture, balance and flexibility as well as aid relaxation.

FITNESS FACTS
- Many people could increase their fitness by just adding a little more exercise to their daily routine.
- We are ten times more likely to continue with a fitness programme if we do something we enjoy, so take up an energetic pastime that you love.
- To improve and maintain your fitness and help weight management, you need to take part in some form of physical activity for 30 minutes on five days a week.
- Stair climbing is a good exercise, so use the stairs in preference to the lift or escalator whenever possible. If you avoid climbing stairs, you are missing an opportunity to get fit and tone your backside!
- Brisk walking over a distance of at least one mile per day is an excellent form of aerobic exercise.
- Use your spare time fruitfully. Look upon your housework, lawn-mowing, your dog walking, digging and DIY as a workout – and do more!

The best exercise for weight loss

Quite simply, if you want to lose weight faster your exercise needs to make you sweat a little and a bit out of breath and you need to exercise for 30 minutes on five days a week. It doesn't have to be done in one session – three sessions of 10 minutes in a day is still very worthwhile. If you watch your calorie intake and combine your aerobic activity with some body conditioning work for, say, 10 minutes on three days a week, you will soon be the proud owner of a fit, trim, shapely and healthy body and one that HELPS you to stay slim by being an efficient fat burner because it's fit!

My *Shape Up & Salsacise* DVD has been designed to accompany this Gi Jeans Diet book. It includes two salsacise workouts (one for beginners and one which is more advanced) plus two fabulous 10-minute tone-up sections to help you target your problem areas: upper body and abs, and hips and thighs. The use of a resistance band makes the exercises significantly more effective. If you practise these workouts regularly you will be amazed at the results (see back of book for further details).

Do read the chapter on exercise later in this book to gain even more understanding of how you can maximise your weight-loss progress and improve your body shape.

7 Find the right weight-loss formula for YOU

What sort of dieter are you? Do you like strict instructions or do you like to make your own choices? The key to weight-loss success is finding the right help for you!

Everyone knows that in order to lose weight you have to eat less food and do more activity. But how you go about it is not quite so straightforward. If you try to lose weight by following a programme that doesn't suit your mentality, you are likely to fail. So let's see how you can avoid failing by finding a formula that suits YOU.

The prescriptive dieter

You like decision-making to be kept to a minimum. 'Just tell me what to eat and I'll do it,' you say. You are happy to weigh out your portions, and you don't snack or cheat. You have very strong willpower. If you follow the diet instructions exactly, you are likely to be the person who loses the most weight in the class or in your clan of colleagues all trying to slim down for your holidays. If you are one of these 'model dieters', there is no doubt you will achieve your goals fast!

RECOMMENDATION: Follow the Gi Jeans Diet and, if possible, join a Rosemary Conley Club and enjoy the encouragement and admiration of the rest of the class. You are likely to win 'Slimmer of the Week' more than most other people.

The diet rebel

You hate being told what to eat and when. 'I do not want to follow a diet. I can't be bothered to weigh food or count calories.' Many people fall into this category and it's OK to want greater freedom in your food choices. The key here is to understand what made you overweight in the first place. Do you eat too much chocolate? Do you drink too much alcohol? Are you totally inactive? Are you a snacker? Do you just eat too much?

RECOMMENDATION: Start by writing down everything you eat and drink for seven days. Be honest. Then look back over the week's consumption and see where you have eaten foods that were 'extras' over and above your mealtimes. Check out the Traffic Light guide in the No Diet Gi Jeans Diet (see pages 98–101) and see how many foods from the Red list you eat regularly. Can you recognise how much fatty food you have been eating in the past? A little? A lot? See where you can make some small changes by selecting more foods from the Green and Amber lists and fewer from the Red.

What can you do to 'spend' some extra calories by being a little more active? Even small changes can turn your life around. Try the Fitness Quiz on pages 251–3 to see which activity is likely to suit you best. Also consider my online slimming club www.slimwithRosemary.com as it is designed for people just like you. It provides a behavioural change programme where you are in control of making some tiny changes that can make a big difference.

The gourmet dieter

You love food and you adore cooking. That is great because you can be in total control of what you eat and can cook it the low-fat way to minimise the calories yet maximise the pleasure.

RECOMMENDATION: The key to your dieting success is being aware of the calories in each recipe, watching your portion sizes, not finishing up the leftovers and not doing too much tasting during preparation. Never start cooking when you are really hungry, and always have some chopped vegetables to nibble on to keep your mouth occupied! The recipes included in this book are made for you and you will have great fun trying them all out. If you are likely to be eating the greatest number of calories in your evening meal, make sure you cut back a little in your other meals by having a little less cereal at breakfast, a lower-calorie sandwich at lunchtime, and avoid snacking apart from two Power Snacks, one mid-morning and one mid-afternoon, and a daily treat allowed on my Gi Jeans Diet.

When shopping for food, make a list of what you need and stick to it. Do not buy any extras just because they are on special offer. You will end up forcing yourself to eat them before they go past their use by date!

The lazy cook dieter

So you don't like cooking? That's fine, too. There are many low-fat, calorie-counted, healthy meals on the supermarket shelves that there is no reason why you shouldn't be able to eat really well. However, do try to balance your intake of processed foods with freshly prepared options for some of your meals during the day or include fresh vegetables or salad accompaniments with your ready meal.

RECOMMENDATION: Now you know which types of foods have a low Gi, try to choose wisely and, when possible, look for products with a low-Gi label and familiarise yourself with your supermarket's low-fat food range. Check the nutrition details on the packaging and only select foods with 5% or less fat content. Whether it is saturated or unsaturated fat is immaterial if you are trying to lose weight.

Next, make sure you are aware of the total calories in the portion you are likely to eat and include this in your daily total. As a quick guideline, allow 200 calories for breakfast, 300 for lunch, 500 for your main meal, 200 calories for 450ml (¾ pint) milk on cereals and in tea and coffee, 50 calories each for two Power Snacks, 100 calories for a daily treat that does not have to be low fat or low Gi, and 100 calories for alcohol. Make sure you include five portions of fruit and/or vegetables in your meal choices and daily calorie allowance.

When buying ready meals, check if you need an accompaniment such as rice, pasta or vegetables and make sure you include the calories for these in your calculations. To keep the Gi rating down, remember to choose basmati rice in preference to other types, pasta in preference to potatoes, or waxy new potatoes instead of old ones.

Work out your own menu planner and write down the calories in each meal/product. After a while, you will know automatically which combinations equal the desired calories.

The active dieter

You love your food and would rather do more exercise to compensate for the extra food you like to eat, but you still want to lose weight.

RECOMMENDATION: Enjoying being active is a great start but you have to do a lot of exercise to lose weight without making some changes to your food intake. If you are able to reduce the fat content of the foods you eat, then increasing your activity levels will speed up your progress.

Carbohydrates (bread, rice, pasta, potatoes and cereal) give you lots of physical energy to exercise, so have a good portion of carbohydrate with each of your three daily meals, bearing in mind the low-Gi guidelines. Protein foods (meat, fish, eggs, low-fat cheese and milk) help renewal and maintenance of your body tissue, particularly if you exercise a lot, but you don't need to eat too much of it. A small to moderate portion at each meal is best, for instance milk with your cereal, ham or chicken in your lunchtime sandwich and maybe lean minced beef spaghetti bolognese for dinner. Keep fat intake to a minimum, otherwise the fat in your diet will only replace the fat that you burn off through exercise. Fruit and vegetables also provide essential vitamins and minerals, so make sure you eat your five portions a day and it's essential to drink plenty of water to prevent dehydration, particularly when exercising.

Try attending your local Rosemary Conley Club once a week. All the instructors are qualified in nutrition and will direct you to the best diet for your needs, plus you will have the discipline of being weighed each week so that you can track your progress. And don't think these classes will be too easy for you if you are already fit – all the instructors are specially trained to teach a wide variety of abilities in the same class so that each individual receives a great workout at the ideal level for them.

8 How to use the Gi Jeans Diet programme

The Gi Jeans Diet is divided into two parts. Part 1 is the Gi Jeans Kick-start Diet, which is quite strict but lasts for only two weeks. It is designed to give an initial boost to your weight loss campaign, which will then motivate you to carry on.

In week three, you move on to Part 2 of the Gi Jeans Diet, which has a much more generous calorie allowance. It allows you to drink alcohol, have two low-fat, low-Gi Power Snacks each day and a daily treat worth 100 calories, which can be anything you like as it is outside the low-fat and low-Gi guidelines. And the good news is that you can save up your treats over several days to accommodate a social occasion or special event. This versatility enables the diet to fit in with your lifestyle and gives you ultimate freedom while you reduce your weight and discover the new, slimmer you that's dying to get out!

No need to count calories, fat or Gi values

All the meal suggestions are calorie-counted, Gi aware and low in fat. Each meal category states the calorie allowance and you can choose which meals you like, repeat your favourites and avoid those that don't take your fancy.

This diet will work best if you are happy with what you are eating. If you really cannot face a high-fibre, natural grain cereal every morning and feel you could only survive on the diet by eating your favourite cereal for breakfast, for instance a high-Gi one such as Crunchy Nut Cornflakes, then have it. The idea is to incorporate more low-Gi foods into your daily diet than you used to so that your overall diet is much healthier. Even if you substitute your own meal ideas in place of the ones listed, so long as you stick to the calorie allowance and observe the 5% fat rule, the diet will still work.

Eating low-Gi foods alone will not make you lose weight faster, but it will keep you feeling fuller for longer so you are less likely to snack. The low-fat, low-Gi Power Snacks that are allowed mid-morning and mid-afternoon each day are designed to stave off hunger pangs so that your tendency to snack throughout the day on high-fat foods such as chocolates, crisps and biscuits can be controlled, which will enable you to stay on track.

Lose weight faster

Remember, if you want to see fast results and watch your skin shrink back and your muscle tone reappear, you will need to take some form or physical activity or exercise each day. This needn't be arduous or excessive – it is just about being on the go more and sitting down watching TV less. It is important for you to understand which exercise does what and that is covered in chapter 6. If you haven't already read this, please take the time to do so if you are serious about achieving a fit and healthy body.

Lifestyle changes

The only way you are going to manage to lose your excess weight and keep it off in the long term is by re-educating your eating habits and making some lifestyle changes that will really help you stay fit and slim without a huge amount of effort. This is not a 'boot camp' regimen. It is an easy, effective and enjoyable journey towards a new you!

Get started

So, you are ready to start the Gi Jeans Kick-start Diet. Read through it carefully to understand how it works and what foods you need to purchase (and which ones you don't!).

The results from my trial dieters (see chapter 18) should give you all the encouragement you need to give it your best shot. Weight losses of up to 12lb in the first two weeks were not uncommon, although 7.25lb was the average. Can you imagine what a difference that could make to how your clothes fit? I hope you enjoy the results.

Reading nutrition labels

The nutrition label on each food product we buy provides a breakdown of its nutritional content as well as the number of calories and amount of fat. To simplify matters, as far as weight control is concerned, the two key things to look at are the 'energy' and the 'fat' values.

The figure relating to 'energy' tells you the number of calories (kcal) in 100g of the product (you can ignore the kj figure). You then need to calculate how much of the product you will actually be eating to work out the number of **calories per portion.**

NUTRITIONAL INFORMATION

	Per 100g
ENERGY	172kj/40 kcal
PROTEIN	1.8g
CARBOHYDRATE (of which are sugars)	8.0g (2.0g)
FAT (of which saturates)	0.2g (Trace)
FIBRE	1.5g
SODIUM	0.3g

The fat content may be broken down into polyunsaturated and saturated but, for anyone on a weight-reducing diet, it is the total fat content per 100g that is the most significant. Remember, when following my Gi Jeans Diet you should only select foods where the label shows the fat content as 5g or less per 100g weight of product, i.e. 5% or less fat. The actual amount of fat per portion is of lesser importance. If you follow the simple 5% fat rule and restrict your calorie intake to around 1400–1500 calories a day for women and 1700–2000 calories a day for men, the fat content of your food will look after itself. The only exceptions to this rule are lean cuts of meat, lamb and pork which may be just over the 5% yardstick, some brands of multigrain bread, and oily fish, such as salmon, herrings and mackerel. These exceptions are made because of the important nutrients they contain that are vital for good health.

Remember that, although the 5% rule is the ideal while you are trying to lose weight, I accept that you might crave a high-fat treat or dine out and are unable to control what foods you eat. That's why I have included a daily treat, which can be outside the low-fat, low-Gi guidelines and which can be saved up if you wish for a special occasion. The occasional high-fat treat is not a disaster. The key is to enjoy it and not to resort to a binge. Just try to balance the calories.

9 The Gi Jeans Kick-start Diet

Follow this Kick-start Diet for two weeks only to give you a head start in your weight-loss campaign. Remember to cook and serve all foods without adding fat. Grill or dry-fry foods instead of frying (or use a little spray oil) and cook vegetables, rice and pasta in water with a vegetable stock cube for added flavour.

What to do

Each day, select one breakfast, lunch and dinner menu. You can repeat any of the menu options as you wish to suit your taste and lifestyle. You should also consume 450ml (¾ pint) skimmed or semi-skimmed milk. If you prefer, you may substitute a low-fat, low-calorie yogurt (max. 75 calories) for 150ml (¼ pint) milk. Tea and coffee can be drunk freely, using milk from your allowance

In addition to the breakfast, lunch and dinner menus you are allowed two extra pieces of fruit as Power Snacks. These Power Snacks should be eaten mid-morning and mid-afternoon even if you are not hungry. You are also allowed 1 × 175g (6oz) extra portion of salad each day, which can be eaten with lunch or dinner or as a separate snack at suppertime if you prefer.

For good health, aim to incorporate five portions of vegetables and/or fruit each day in your daily allowance. These will also help fill you up.

During this two-week Gi Jeans Kick-start Diet do not drink any alcohol but do drink at least five large glasses of water each day. Don't worry – after the two weeks are completed you can drink alcohol again!

I always recommend that anyone who follows a weight-reducing diet take a multi-vitamin supplement but it is particularly important during this stricter two-week diet.

So to recap, each day you can have:

> 1 breakfast, 1 lunch and 1 dinner
> 1 extra portion of salad
> 2 extra pieces of fruit (Power Snacks)
> 450ml (¾ pint) skimmed or semi-skimmed milk
> 5 large glasses of water
> Unlimited tea and coffee

Diet notes

Low fat

The term 'low fat' refers to any product with 5% or less fat.

Bread

For ease of reference within the diet plan, 1 slice should weigh 40g (1½oz) and contain a maximum of 90 calories.

Fruit

'1 piece fruit' means one apple, one pear, etc., or 115g (4oz) fruit such as grapes, strawberries, etc. For the purposes of this diet, one banana counts as two pieces. Choose slightly under-ripe rather than over-ripe ones for a lower Gi rating.

Drinks

Drink plenty of water, at least 5 large glasses a day. Low-calorie drinks are also unrestricted. Don't drink any alcohol for the two weeks of the Gi Jeans Kick-start Diet. Tea and coffee may be drunk freely, using milk from your allowance.

Milk

Milk can be skimmed or semi-skimmed, cow's, goat's or soya milk. If you find 450ml (¾ pint) is too much, you can always substitute a low-fat yogurt in place of 150ml (¼ pint) milk. This can be eaten as a dessert or as a between-meal snack if you wish.

Breakfasts

Approx. 200 kcal each

CEREAL BREAKFASTS

- Ⓥ 40g (1½oz) any whole-oat or high-fibre cereal with 1 tsp sugar and milk from allowance; 1 piece fruit
- Ⓥ 20g (¾oz) any whole-oat or high-fibre cereal served with artificial sugar substitute and milk from allowance; 1 × 100g pot low-fat fruit yogurt (max. 75 kcal) and 1 piece fruit
- Ⓥ 20g (¾oz) Special K cereal served with milk from allowance; ½ slice toasted multigrain bread spread with Marmite and topped with 10 cherry tomatoes; 1 piece fruit
- Ⓥ 25g (1oz) muesli mixed with 100g (3½oz) 0% fat Greek-style yogurt
- Ⓥ 40g (1½oz) porridge oats cooked in water and served with milk from allowance and 1 tsp runny honey or sugar

Ⓥ means suitable for vegetarians or vegetarian option is available.

FRUIT BREAKFASTS

- Ⓥ 1 large banana, peeled and sliced, served with 1 pot low-fat yogurt, any flavour (max. 75 kcal)
- Ⓥ Gi fruit salad comprising 1 satsuma, broken into segments, 1 pear, finely chopped with skin intact, 25g (1oz) seedless grapes and 15g (½oz) oats mixed with 2 tbsps 0% fat Greek-style yogurt (e.g. Total 0%)
- Ⓥ 225g (8oz) fresh fruit topped with 2 tbsps 0% fat Greek-style yogurt (e.g. Total 0%)
- Ⓥ 2 pieces fruit plus 1 medium banana or 1 pot low-fat yogurt (max. 100 kcal)

QUICK AND EASY BREAKFASTS

- Ⓥ 1 slice toasted multigrain bread spread with 2 tsps honey or marmalade; 1 piece fruit
- Ⓥ ½ fresh grapefruit sprinkled with low-calorie sweetener if desired; 1 medium-sized boiled egg served with ½ slice toasted multigrain bread spread with Marmite; 1 piece fruit
- 1 slice multigrain bread spread with savoury sauce, e.g. tomato ketchup, fruity sauce, etc., and topped with 2 grilled turkey rashers; 1 piece fruit
- Ⓥ 1 × 35g Rosemary Conley Low Gi Nutrition Bar; 1 low-fat yogurt (max. 85 kcal)

Lunches

Approx. 250 kcal each

SANDWICH AND SALAD LUNCHES

- Ⓥ 2 slices multigrain bread spread with low-calorie salad dressing and filled with unlimited salad plus 25g (1oz) salmon or mackerel or wafer thin ham/chicken/beef or 50g (2oz) low-fat cottage cheese
- Ⓥ 1 medium pitta bread split open and filled with lettuce plus either: 50g (2oz) tuna (in brine) or salmon mixed with 25g (1oz) canned sweetcorn; or 75g (3oz) low-fat cottage cheese and 1 tsp fat-free dressing
- Ⓥ Any prepacked low-fat sandwich (made with multigrain bread) or pasta salad (max. 250 kcal)
- 50g (2oz) salmon, mackerel or trout served with 1 tsp horseradish sauce and a large salad; 1 medium banana
- Ⓥ 350g (12oz) chopped salad vegetables with soy sauce or balsamic vinegar to taste, plus 1 chicken drumstick (all skin removed) or 1 small (205g) can baked beans or 50g (2oz) salmon or mackerel
- Prawn and Pasta Salad (see recipe, page 119)
- 50g (2oz) wafer thin pastrami/ham/chicken/beef/turkey or 75g (3oz) low-fat cottage cheese served with Potato and Watercress Salad (see recipe, page 123)
- Ⓥ 50g (2oz) low-fat cottage cheese served with Courgette and Red Onion Salad (see recipe, page 120)
- Curried Chicken and Pasta Salad (see recipe, page 125)
- Potted Smoked Trout (see recipe, page 170) served with Crunchy Green Gi Salad (see recipe, page 119)

COOKED LUNCHES

- 1 slice toasted multigrain bread topped with 1 poached or dry-fried egg, plus 3 grilled tomatoes
- Ⓥ Super-quick stir-fry: preheat a non-stick pan or wok till hot. Add 150g (5oz) chicken breast or 225g (8oz) Quorn chunks and plenty of freshly ground black pepper and dry-fry until thoroughly cooked. Add 350g (12oz) chopped vegetables (ideally include some beansprouts) and dry-fry until hot. Sprinkle with 2 tbsps soy sauce and toss to lightly coat the vegetables. Serve immediately
- Ⓥ 1 can any low-fat soup (max. 150 kcal) served with 1 slice plain or toasted multigrain bread
- Gingered Carrot Soup (see recipe, page 115) served with 1 small multigrain roll
- Creamy Red Lentil Soup (see recipe, page 118); 1 piece fruit
- Ⓥ Three Pepper Frittata (see recipe, page 190) served with 3 grilled tomatoes and a small green salad
- Ⓥ Peppers Stuffed with Wild Mushrooms (see recipe, page 221) served with salad and 1 small multigrain roll; 1 low-fat yogurt (max. 70 kcal)
- Ⓥ Italian Toast Toppers (see recipe, page 189)
- Ⓥ Tomato and Pepper Pasta (see recipe, page 217)
- Ⓥ Stir-fry Quorn (see recipe, page 195) served with 40g (1½oz) [uncooked weight] boiled basmati rice

Quick guide to Rice

35g (1oz) [uncooked weight] basmati rice weighs 75g (3oz), equivalent to 2½ tbsps, when cooked.

Dinners

Approx. 400 kcal each

MEAT DINNERS

- 3 low-fat sausages served with 175g (6oz) new potatoes (with skins) and unlimited other vegetables
- 115g (4oz) any lean meat, grilled, roasted or dry-fried, served with 115g (4oz) new potatoes (with skins), unlimited other vegetables and low-fat gravy
- Crunchy Bacon Spaghetti (see recipe, page 147) plus Crunchy Green Gi Salad (see recipe, page 119)
- Pan-fried Liver with Onions and Balsamic Vinegar (see recipe, page 155) served with 50g (2oz) new potatoes (with skins) and unlimited green vegetables
- Beef with Green Vegetables Stir-fry (see recipe, page 139) served with 50g (2oz) [uncooked weight] boiled basmati rice
- Lamb Burgers (see recipe, page 153) served with 100g (3½oz) new potatoes (with skins) plus vegetables
- Teriyaki Pork with Spinach (see recipe, page 142) served with 100g (3½oz) boiled new potatoes (with skins) and unlimited vegetables
- Pork and Mango Meatballs with Chilli Sauce (see recipe, page 143) served with 100g (3½oz) boiled new potatoes (with skins) plus unlimited vegetables
- Creamy Tomato and Sage Pork Steaks (see recipe, page 145) with 100g (3½oz) new potatoes plus vegetables
- Beef Stroganoff (see recipe, page 132) served with 50g (2oz) [uncooked weight] boiled basmati rice

POULTRY DINNERS

- 1 × 200g (7oz) grilled or baked chicken portion served with Creamy Lemon Broad Beans (see recipe, page 222)
- Chicken stir-fry (serves 1): dry-fry 175g (6oz) chopped chicken breast with plenty of freshly ground black pepper in a preheated non-stick pan or wok until almost cooked. Add ½ chopped onion and 3 mushrooms, 1 chopped celery stick, ½ coarsely chopped red or green pepper and cook lightly. Add 2 tbsps soy sauce and toss all the ingredients together. Serve with 40g (1½oz) [uncooked weight] boiled basmati rice mixed with 1 × 175g (6oz) can beansprouts (place cooked rice and beansprouts into a colander and pour boiling water over to heat through)
- Spicy Chicken Pasta (see recipe, page 159) served with unlimited vegetables (excluding potatoes) or salad
- Chicken curry (serves 4): 4 × 175g (4 × 6oz) chop chicken breasts and dry-fry in a non-stick pan or wok. Add 1 large chopped onion and cook until soft. Add 1 × 450g jar any low-fat Indian curry sauce with crispy vegetables, cover and simmer for 15 minutes. Serve with 50g (2oz) [uncooked] boiled basmati rice per person
- Turkey and Pepper Stroganoff (see recipe, page 165) served with 50g (2oz) [uncooked weight] boiled basmati rice
- Any branded low-fat pasta ready meal with chicken or turkey (max. 350 kcal) served with unlimited vegetables (excluding potatoes)

FISH AND SEAFOOD DINNERS

- 175g (6oz) any white fish, grilled, baked or microwaved, served with 175g (6oz) boiled new potatoes (with skins) and other vegetables plus 1 tbsp low-fat sauce of your choice
- Fisherman's Pie (see recipe, page 174) served with unlimited vegetables (excluding potatoes)
- Smoked Ham and Prawn Jambalya (see recipe, page 183) served with Crunchy Green Gi Salad (see recipe, page 119)
- Tuna and Tarragon Pasta (see recipe, page 181)
- Any branded low-fat pasta ready meal with fish/seafood (max. 350 kcal) served with unlimited vegetables (excluding potatoes)
- 1 × 115g (4oz) salmon steak, grilled or steamed, served with 100g (3½oz) boiled new potatoes (with skins) and unlimited green vegetables
- Pan-fried Tuna with Pepper Noodles (see recipe, page 171) served with unlimited vegetables (excluding potatoes)
- Blackened Tuna with Honey and Ginger Beansprouts (see recipe, page 179) served with 100g (3½oz) boiled new potatoes (with skins) and unlimited vegetables
- Baked Halibut Steak with Sage and Parma Ham (see recipe, page 170) served with 115g (4oz) boiled new potatoes (with skins) and unlimited other vegetables
- Spicy Prawn Masala (see recipe, page 184) plus 50g (2oz) [uncooked weight] boiled basmati rice and a large mixed salad

VEGETARIAN DINNERS

- Ⓥ Mediterranean Stuffed Peppers (see recipe, page 197) served with 50g (2oz) [uncooked weight] boiled basmati rice and unlimited salad or vegetables
- Ⓥ Lentil and Potato Pie (see recipe, page 218) served with unlimited vegetables (excluding potatoes)
- Ⓥ Summer Vegetable Bake (see recipe, page 220) served with Peppers Stuffed with Wild Mushrooms (see recipe, page 221) or unlimited vegetables or salad
- Ⓥ Butter Bean Hotpot (see recipe, page 200) served with unlimited vegetables
- Ⓥ 4 Quorn sausages served with 175g (6oz) boiled new potatoes (with skins) and unlimited vegetables
- Ⓥ Quorn stir-fry (serves 1): dry-fry 225g (8oz) Quorn chunks with plenty of freshly ground black pepper in a preheated non-stick pan or wok until almost cooked. Add ½ chopped onion, 3 mushrooms, 1 chopped celery stick, ½ coarsely chopped red or green pepper and cook lightly. Add 2 tbsps soy sauce and toss well. Serve with 40g (1½oz) [uncooked weight] boiled basmati rice mixed with 1 × 175g (6oz) can beansprouts
- Ⓥ 2-egg omelette cooked (without fat) with chopped peppers, onion, mushrooms, peas, tomatoes, herbs and black pepper, plus 175g (6oz) boiled new potatoes
- Ⓥ Sweet Potato, Pepper and Fennel Bake (see recipe, page 194) served with unlimited vegetables (excluding potatoes)
- Ⓥ Any low-fat vegetarian ready meal (max. 350 kcal) served with unlimited vegetables (excluding potatoes)

10 The Gi Jeans Diet: Part 2

If you have managed to stick strictly to the Gi Jeans Kick-start Diet you have done well. You can now enjoy more food as well as a daily alcoholic drink. In addition to this you can have two Power Snacks each day plus a daily treat that is free of the Gi and low-fat guidelines. That means it can be high in Gi and high in fat so that you never feel forbidden from eating your favourite foods. If you want to eat a bar of chocolate or bag of crisps, you can. Just make sure that you have the equivalent number of calories saved up within your daily allowance.

Part 2 of the Gi Jeans Diet is based on 1500 calories a day of low-fat, low- or medium-Gi foods. For most people who are overweight this is the optimum calorie allowance to effect a healthy rate of weight loss while giving you plenty to eat and the freedom to have a drink and a treat each day. If you follow the diet strictly and combine it with regular exercise, you should lose 2– 2½lb or 1 kilo of body fat each week. Those who are significantly overweight can eat more calories and still achieve this rate of weight loss. For those who have only a few pounds to lose you may find progress slower as your calorie expenditure will obviously be less because there is less of you.

The ideal is to eat the number of calories equal to your basal metabolic rate (BMR) – that's the number of calories you would burn each day if you just stayed in bed and did nothing. This amount of daily food will satisfy your basic energy requirement. Then every bit of activity you do all day, from getting out of bed and going about your daily routine, will use energy from the fat stores deposited around your body and you will lose weight. Check the BMR charts on pages 312–5 to find out your personal calorie allowance. If your daily allowance is greater than 1500, you can increase your portion sizes accordingly, for instance by increasing your portion of rice, pasta or potatoes or by having an extra Power Snack or piece of fruit each day. As you lose weight you can adjust your calorie allowance to ensure that your rate of weight loss is maintained.

If you have a lot of weight to lose, please be cautious about cutting back on the calories too soon as this could make reaching your ultimate goal much harder. It is in your short- and long-term interests to keep your metabolic rate buoyant. Eating the optimum number of calories to meet your basal metabolic rate is by far the best way to achieve results.

As we get older our metabolic rate slows down so we need fewer daily calories. If we don't reduce the calories as we get older, we can gain weight very easily. If you are aged over 60, you may find it easier to stick with the Gi Jeans Kick-start Diet, which is based on 1200 calories a day. Alternatively, you could still follow Part 2 of the diet but exclude the alcohol allowance and the treat. Because all the meals and snacks are calorie counted it is simple to make your own selections or substitutions.

In the diet menus that follow you should find plenty of options to suit your taste and your lifestyle. See also the Busy Day Menu Plan on pages 96–7. So, just follow the rules, select foods you enjoy and wait for the results.

What to do

Each day you can have:

450ml (¾ pint) skimmed or semi-skimmed milk	200 kcal
Breakfast	200 kcal
Lunch	300 kcal
Dinner	500 kcal
2 Power Snacks	100 kcal
1 Treat	100 kcal
1 Alcoholic drink	100 kcal
Total	1500 kcal

'FREE' CALORIES

- Tea and coffee (drunk black or with milk from allowance)
- Water
- Sugar-free soft drinks
- Chopped raw vegetables: cucumber, peppers, carrots, onions, mushrooms, celery and courgettes
- You may take a multi-vitamin supplement each day if you wish

Diet notes

Low fat

The term 'low fat' refers to any product with 5% or less fat content.

Bread

Bread should be stoneground or multigrain (max. 90 calories per slice). Some brands have more than 5% fat and these are acceptable on this Gi Jeans Diet because of their nutritional qualities. For ease of reference, one slice should weigh 40g (1½oz).

Breakfast cereals

Choose whole-oat or high-fibre varieties, e.g. All-Bran, Fruit 'n Fibre, Bran Buds, Grapenuts, muesli, Shredded Wheat, and Weetabix. Special K is also good as it contains valuable nutrients.

Salad

'Salad' includes all salad leaves, cress, tomatoes, cucumber, and chopped raw vegetables such as carrots, peppers, onions, mushrooms, celery and courgettes. You may serve it with 1 tsp fat-free, low-calorie dressing.

Fruit and vegetables

'1 piece fruit' means one apple, one pear, etc., or 115g (4oz) fruit such as strawberries, etc. For the purposes of this diet, one banana counts as two pieces. Choose under-ripe rather than over-ripe ones for a lower Gi rating. For good health, aim to incorporate at least five portions a day of fruit and/or vegetables in your menu selections.

Milk

Milk can be skimmed or semi-skimmed, cow's, goat's or soya milk. If 450ml (¾ pint) is too much, you can substitute a low-fat yogurt in place of 150ml (¼ pint) milk. This can be eaten as a dessert or as a between-meal snack.

Drinks

Drink plenty of water, at least five large glasses a day. Tea and coffee may be drunk freely using milk from your allowance. You may also drink unlimited low-calorie soft drinks.

Alcohol

Women may have 100 calories of alcohol per day and men 200 calories. You can save up your allowance for a special occasion if you wish.

Sugar

If you prefer to have more sugar on your cereal than is included in the diet plan, use a granulated low-calorie alternative.

Rosemary Conley products

We are developing a range of healthy, low-fat, low-Gi foods that will be available in several supermarkets. Rosemary Conley low-fat mousses are currently sold in Asda, Tesco, and Co op, and the Low Gi Nutrition Bar in Tesco only. The range is constantly being updated. For information on new products and where they can be purchased, visit the Rosemary Conley website (www.rosemary-conley.co.uk).

Ⓥ means suitable for vegetarians or vegetarian option is available.

Breakfasts

Approx. 200 kcal each

CEREAL BREAKFASTS

- Ⓥ Any cereal breakfast from the Gi Jeans Kick-start diet menu
- Ⓥ 1 Weetabix served with 1 tsp sugar and milk from allowance; 1 large banana
- Ⓥ 50g (2oz) All-Bran served with milk from allowance, topped with 115g (4oz) strawberries and 1 tsp sugar
- Ⓥ 50g (2oz) Special K cereal served with milk from allowance and 1 tsp sugar
- Ⓥ 2 Shredded Wheat sprinkled with 1 grated apple and served with milk from allowance and 1 tsp sugar
- Ⓥ 40g (1½oz) muesli served with milk from allowance and 1 tsp brown sugar

FRUIT BREAKFASTS

- Ⓥ Any fruit breakfast from the Gi Jeans Kick-start diet menu
- Ⓥ 1 medium banana and 115g (4oz) strawberries or raspberries sliced and stirred into 1 × 100g pot low-fat yogurt (max. 75 kcal)
- Ⓥ 10 prunes in natural juice and 2 tbsps low-fat yogurt
- Ⓥ 4 pieces fruit (excluding bananas)
- Ⓥ 225g (8oz) mixed fresh berries (e.g. blueberries, raspberries, etc.) topped with 2 tbsps 0% fat Greek-style yogurt (e.g. Total 0%)

COOKED BREAKFASTS

- 2 grilled low-fat sausages served with 150g (5oz) tomatoes (grilled tomatoes or canned tomatoes) and 100g (3½oz) grilled mushrooms

- 1 poached or dry-fried egg served with 1 low-fat sausage, 4 grilled tomatoes and 115g (4oz) grilled mushrooms

- 2 grilled turkey rashers served with 2 large grilled tomatoes, 115g (4oz) grilled mushrooms and 50g (2oz) dry-fried sliced onions plus 1 slice toasted multigrain bread

- Ⓥ 1 slice toasted multigrain bread spread with 2 tsps honey or marmalade; 1 piece fruit

- 1 slice multigrain bread spread with savoury sauce, e.g. tomato ketchup, fruity sauce, etc., and topped with 2 grilled turkey rashers; 1 piece fruit

- Ⓥ Pizza toastie: 1 slice toasted multigrain bread covered with sliced ripe tomatoes, topped with 50g (2oz) sliced half-fat mozzarella cheese and grilled until melted; 115g (4oz) fresh raspberries or strawberries served with 1 low-fat yogurt (max. 75 kcal)

- Ⓥ 40g (1½oz) porridge oats cooked in water. Served with milk from allowance and 1 tsp honey or sugar

- Ⓥ ½ fresh grapefruit sprinkled with low-calorie sweetener if desired; 1 medium-sized boiled egg served with ½ slice toasted multigrain bread spread with Marmite; 1 piece fruit

- Ⓥ 1 slice multigrain bread toasted and topped with 3 tbsps baked beans and 2 sliced tomatoes

Lunches

Approx. 300 kcal each

SANDWICHES, ROLLS AND WRAPS

- BLT: 1 small multigrain roll spread with reduced-oil salad dressing and filled with 50g (2oz) grilled lean bacon plus sliced tomato and lettuce
- 2 slices multigrain bread spread with 2 tsps horseradish sauce topped with 50g (2oz) pastrami and 4 cherry tomatoes; 1 piece fruit
- Ⓥ 1 small multigrain roll spread with reduced-oil salad dressing and filled with salad plus 25g (1oz) wafer thin ham/chicken/beef/turkey or 50g (2oz) low-fat cottage cheese served with Crunchy Green Gi Salad (see recipe, page 119)
- Ⓥ 2 slices multigrain bread spread with low-fat dressing and filled with salad plus one of the following:
  - 75g (3oz) wafer thin ham/chicken/beef
  - 115g (4oz) low-fat cottage cheese
  - 75g (3oz) tuna canned in brine
  - 50g (2oz) crab meat
  - 50g (2oz) mackerel canned in tomato sauce
- Prawn cocktail open sandwich: mix 115g (4oz) cooked, shelled prawns with 1 heaped tsp low-fat Marie Rose dressing and place on top of 1 slice multigrain bread. Serve with a small salad
- 1 × 50g (2oz) pitta bread filled with 50g (2oz) cooked, skinless chicken breast, sliced, green salad, sliced cherry tomatoes and 1 tbsp reduced-fat guacamole

- Parma ham baguette: cut 1 small multigrain baguette in half and spread with 30g Extra Light Philadelphia. Top with 30g (1¼oz) Parma ham (all fat removed) and fresh basil leaves
- Chilli prawn roll: cut 1 multigrain roll in half and spread each half with 1 triangle Laughing Cow Extra Light Cheese. Mix 1 tbsp sweet chilli sauce with 2 tbsps cooked, shelled prawns and place on top of each half. Add a few rocket or lettuce leaves and season with freshly ground black pepper
- Quick Tuna Pâté (see recipe, page 169) served with 1 slice toasted multigrain bread and salad
- Ⓥ 1 × 50g (2oz) pitta bread split open and filled with crisp green salad leaves, sliced cherry tomatoes, 5 pitted black olives, 25g (1oz) diced feta cheese and 1 tbsp Total 0% fat Greek-style yogurt mixed with chopped mint; 1 piece fruit
- Ⓥ 1 × 50g (2oz) pitta bread split open and filled with shredded lettuce, sliced peppers, spring onions, sliced cherry tomatoes and either 50g (2oz) canned salmon or tuna in brine or low-fat cottage cheese with sweetcorn
- Ⓥ 1 mini pitta bread served with Lemon and Mustard Seed Humous (see recipe, page 186); 1 piece fruit
- Ⓥ Grilled Pepper and Herb Pittas (see recipe, page 188)
- Ⓥ Sweetcorn and Pepper Fajitas (see recipe, page 187); 1 piece fruit
- Ⓥ Any prepacked low-fat sandwich made with multigrain bread (max. 300 kcal)

SALAD LUNCHES

- ⓥ Any salad from the Gi Jeans Kick-start lunch menu plus 1 piece fruit
- ⓥ Cheese and coleslaw salad: mix together 115g (4oz) low-fat cottage cheese and 115g (4oz) low-fat coleslaw. Season with black pepper and serve with baby beetroot, sliced cucumber and cherry tomatoes plus 1 slice multigrain bread
- 1 × 100g (3½oz) can pink salmon in brine, drained, mixed with salad leaves, sliced peppers, cucumber chunks, spring onions and cherry tomatoes tossed in oil-free dressing. Serve with 1 small multigrain roll; 1 peach or nectarine
- 50g (2oz) smoked mackerel fillet served with 1 tsp horseradish sauce and a large mixed salad tossed in oil-free dressing plus 1 slice multigrain bread
- Warm Steak and Blue Cheese Salad (see recipe, page 129)
- Lemon Seafood Salad (see recipe, page 130) served with 1 slice multigrain bread
- Chicken Caesar Salad (see recipe, page 128) served with 1 small multigrain roll; 1 piece fruit
- Coronation Chicken (see recipe, page 127) served with Crunchy Green Gi Salad (see recipe, page 119)
- ⓥ Mixed Bean Salad with Balsamic Vinegar and Lime (see recipe, page 124); 1 medium banana
- ⓥ Cucumber and White Bean Salad (see recipe, page 122) served with 1 small multigrain roll
- Chicken Couscous Salad (see recipe, page 121)

COOKED LUNCHES

- ⓥ Any cooked lunch from the Gi Jeans Kick-start Diet menu plus 1 piece fruit
- ⓥ Creamy Red Lentil Soup (see recipe, page 118) served with 1 small multigrain roll
- Thyme-flavoured White Bean Soup (see recipe, page 117) served with 1 slice multigrain bread; 1 piece fruit
- ⓥ Cauliflower and Stilton Soup (see recipe, page 116) served with 1 slice multigrain bread
- ⓥ Black Bean Soup (see recipe, page 114)
- ⓥ Baked Ginger Stuffed Tomatoes (see recipe, page 191) served with 1 small multigrain roll
- ⓥ Vegetable stir-fry: dissolve a vegetable stock cube in a pan of boiling water. Add 50g (2oz) [uncooked weight] basmati rice and cook for 10 minutes. Preheat a non-stick frying pan or wok and sprinkle with freshly ground black pepper. Add a selection chopped vegetables, e.g. onions, peppers, mushrooms, celery, chilli, courgettes. Stir frequently and, when almost cooked, add a sachet of Blue Dragon stir-fry sauce of your choice. Drain the rice and serve with the vegetable stir-fry
- ⓥ 1 × 175g (6oz) cooked jacket potato topped with 1 small can (205g) baked beans and served with a large salad
- Broccoli and Smoked Salmon Spaghetti (see recipe, page 168)
- ⓥ Tofu and Pepper Stir-fry with Rice (see recipe, page 193)

- Ⓥ Tomato and Lemon Penne (see recipe, page 208) served with a large mixed salad
- Ⓥ Three Pepper Frittata (see recipe, page 190) with unlimited grilled tomatoes and salad; 1 low-fat yogurt (max. 100 kcal and 5% fat) and 75g (3oz) strawberries
- 2 low-fat sausages, grilled, served with 115g (4oz) baked beans, 10 grilled cherry tomatoes and 115g (4oz) grilled mushrooms plus ½ slice toasted multigrain bread
- Ⓥ Pasta in tomato and basil sauce: cook 75g (3½oz) penne pasta in boiling water with a vegetable stock cube. Drain and return to the pan. Add a small jar of tomato and basil cook-in-sauce and add more fresh basil to taste
- Ⓥ Spaghetti Napoletana: dry-fry ½ chopped onion, 1 diced red pepper and 1 crushed garlic clove for 5 minutes. Add 1 small can chopped tomatoes and heat through. Serve with 50g (2oz) [uncooked weight] boiled spaghetti and a sprinkling of Parmesan
- Ⓥ Spicy Chickpea Casserole (see recipe, page 204) served with a large mixed salad; 1 banana
- Ⓥ Creamy Basil Pasta (see recipe, page 209) served with a large mixed salad
- Ⓥ Aubergine Sombrero Pasta (see recipe, page 206) served a small mixed salad
- Ⓥ Hot and Sour Noodle Stir-fry (see recipe, page 203)

FAST AND FILLING LUNCHES

- Ⓥ 1 × 400g can any branded lentil or vegetable soup (max. 200 kcal) served with 1 small multigrain roll
- 1 slice toasted multigrain bread topped with 1 × 205g can baked beans plus salad
- 50g (2oz) smoked mackerel or 75g (3oz) fresh salmon served with 75g (3oz) boiled new potatoes (with skins) and a small salad with fat-free dressing
- Ⓥ Goat's cheese toastie: 2 slices toasted multigrain bread rubbed with fresh garlic and covered with chopped cherry, tomatoes, red onion and fresh herbs. Top with 1 × 15g (½oz) slice goat's cheese and grill
- 150g (5oz) lean cooked chicken breast (no skin) served with a large mixed salad and any oil-free dressing of your choice plus 1 small multigrain roll
- 50g canned tuna (in brine) served with Indonesian Rice (see recipe, page 192) and 1 slice multigrain bread
- Sardines on toast: top 1 slice toasted multigrain bread with 100g (3½oz) sardines in tomato sauce. Sprinkle with balsamic vinegar and a little chopped basil. Place under a hot grill and heat through; 1 piece fruit
- Mix together 1 chopped green pepper, 1 chopped tomato, chopped cucumber, 50g (2oz) [uncooked weight] boiled basmati rice, 25g (1oz) peas and 25g (1oz) sweetcorn. Add soy sauce and black pepper to taste and serve with 115g (4oz) wafer thin ham or beef; 1 piece fruit
- Ⓥ 1 × 205g can baked beans (eaten cold); 1 × 35g Rosemary Conley Low Gi Nutrition Bar plus 1 kiwi fruit

Dinners

Approx. 500 kcal each

Where the calories allow, a dessert has been included in these dinner menus. You can substitute a dessert of your choice, providing you do not exceed the calories available. Where no dessert has been included you can use the 100 calories available from your Treat or Alcohol allowance if you wish.

In addition to the following menus, you may also choose any item from the Gi Jeans Kick-start Diet dinner menu and have it with an extra glass of wine.

BEEF DINNERS

- 115g (4oz) lean fillet or rump steak grilled and served with 115g (4oz) boiled new potatoes (with skins) and unlimited green vegetables plus grilled tomatoes and mushrooms; 1 × 110g Rosemary Conley Belgian Chocolate Mousse or 1 low-fat yogurt or fromage frais (max. 125 kcal)
- Roast Beef with Yorkshire Pudding and Dry-roast Sweet Potatoes (see recipe, page 140) served with unlimited other vegetables
- Beef Olives (see recipe, page 133) served with 150g (5oz) boiled new potatoes (with skins) and unlimited other vegetables
- Fillet Steak with Salsa Verde (see recipe, page 138) served with 100g (3½oz) boiled new potatoes (with skins) and unlimited other vegetables

- Beef and vegetable bolognese: dry-fry 75g (3oz) extra lean minced beef in a non-stick pan or wok until browned. Drain away any fat. Add to the pan 1 small chopped onion, 1 crushed garlic clove, 1 finely sliced carrot and 225g (8oz) sliced mushrooms. Cook for 5 minutes. Add 1 × 200g can tomatoes, 1 pinch of mixed herbs, 1 beef stock cube, crumbled, and a splash of red wine. Season to taste with freshly ground black pepper. Simmer gently until the vegetables are cooked and the sauce has thickened. Serve with 50g (2oz) [uncooked weight] boiled spaghetti and a large salad; 225g (8oz) fresh fruit salad
- Beef Chilli with Beer (see recipe, page 135) served with 50g (2oz) [uncooked weight] boiled basmati rice
- Beef Stroganoff (see recipe, page 132) served with 100g (3½oz) boiled new potatoes (with skins) and unlimited other vegetables
- Spaghetti Bolognese (see recipe, page 134) served with unlimited salad
- Chilli Beef Linguine (see recipe, page 137) served with unlimited salad; Apricot and Cherry Filo Stack (see recipe, page 237)
- Braised Beef Steaks with Wild Mushrooms (see recipe, page 131) served with 100g (3½oz) boiled new potatoes (with skins), unlimited other vegetables and horseradish sauce

LAMB DINNERS

- 1 × 115g (4oz) lamb steak, grilled, served with 115g (4oz) boiled new potatoes (with skins), unlimited other vegetables, mint sauce and low-fat gravy

- Chilli lamb: mix together 1 tbsp chilli sauce, with ½ tbsp each plum sauce, tomato ketchup and water. Place 1 lean lamb steak under a preheated grill for 4–6 minutes each side, turning once. Halfway through cooking the second side, brush the steak with sauce and continue cooking for the final 2-3 minutes. Serve with 50g (2oz) [uncooked weight] boiled basmati rice or pasta, any remaining sauce and a mixed salad; 1 piece fruit

- 175g (6oz) lamb's liver braised with onions in low-fat gravy and served with 115g (4oz) boiled new potatoes (with skins) and unlimited other vegetables; 1 × 220g can pear slices in natural juice

- Rack of Lamb with Garlic Herb Crust (see recipe, page 152) served with 100g (3½oz) Dry-roast Sweet Potatoes (see recipe, page 140) and unlimited green vegetables

- Lamb and Pearl Barley Casserole (see recipe, page 151) served with boiled or steamed cabbage or carrots; 1 low-fat yogurt (max. 75 kcal)

- Lamb Kofta with Creamy Chilli Dip (see recipe, page 154) served with Saffron Couscous Salad (see recipe, page 126) plus a large mixed salad tossed in oil-free dressing

PORK AND GAMMON DINNERS

- 115g (4oz) lean pork steak, grilled, served with apple sauce plus 1 tbsp sage and onion stuffing (made from a packet with water), 115g (4oz) boiled new potatoes (with skins) and unlimited other vegetables
- 2 large low-fat pork sausages well grilled and served with 115g (4oz) boiled new potatoes (with skins) and unlimited other vegetables; Blackberry and Port Ice (see recipe, page 231)
- 4 low-fat pork sausages grilled and served with 100g (3½oz) boiled new or old potatoes, mashed with milk or yogurt and seasoned well, plus 205g baked beans and 10 grilled cherry tomatoes
- Charcoal Pork Slices with Barbecue Sauce (see recipe, page 144) served with 100g (3½oz) boiled new potatoes (with skins) plus a large salad tossed in oil-free dressing
- Chorizo Jambalaya (see recipe, page 149) served with unlimited green vegetables; Moroccan Clementines (see recipe, page 232)
- 1 × 150g (5oz) lean gammon steak grilled and served with 1 tbsp apple sauce, 115g (4oz) boiled new potatoes (with skins) and unlimited green vegetables; 1 low-fat yogurt (max. 100 kcal) and 1 piece fruit
- Gammon with Pineapple Rice (see recipe, page 148) served with a mixed salad
- Pork Fillet stuffed with Apricots (see recipe, page 146) served with unlimited vegetables (excluding potatoes)

POULTRY DINNERS

- 175g (6oz) chicken breast grilled and served with 175g (6oz) boiled new potatoes (with skins) plus unlimited other vegetables and a little low-fat gravy

- 175g (6oz) lean chicken breast, grilled or baked in the oven, and served with Roast Sweet Potatoes with Chilli Glaze (see recipe, page 224) and unlimited green vegetables

- Chicken stir-fry: cut 115g (4oz) chicken breast into strips and dry-fry in a hot non-stick frying pan with plenty of black pepper. When almost cooked, add 1 small crushed garlic clove, 115g (4oz) chopped fresh vegetables (e.g. courgettes, celery, onion, green, red, yellow peppers, mange-tout, carrots and beansprouts). Add a little grated fresh root ginger. Stir in ½ packet any Blue Dragon stir-fry sauce until the chicken and vegetables are well coated and serve immediately with 50g (2oz) [uncooked weight] boiled basmati rice

- Chicken kebabs: cut 150g (5oz) skinless, boneless chicken breast into chunks and thread with green peppers and cherry tomatoes on to a skewer. Brush with soy sauce and place under a hot grill until the chicken is cooked. Serve with 1 tsp satay sauce and 50g (2oz) [uncooked weight] boiled basmati rice or pasta; 1 low-fat yogurt or fromage frais (max. 100 kcal)

- Spicy Chicken Drumsticks (see recipe, page 157) served with Saffron Couscous Salad (see recipe, page 126); 225g (8oz) fresh fruit salad topped with 1 tbsp 0% fat Greek-style yogurt

- 175g (6oz) chicken breast grilled or griddled and served with Red Beans and Rice (see recipe, page 216)
- Curried Chicken and Potato Salad (see recipe, page 125) served with a small mixed salad; Apricot and Cherry Filo Stack (see recipe, page 237)
- Turmeric Chicken (see recipe, page 158) served with 115g (4oz) boiled new potatoes (with skins) and unlimited other vegetables
- Turkey Lasagne (see recipe, page 166) served with a mixed salad
- Chicken Jalfrezi (see recipe, page 160) served with 75g (3oz) [uncooked weight] basmati rice and a green salad
- Chicken with Fresh Wild Mushrooms (see recipe, page 162) served with 115g (4oz) boiled new potatoes (with skins) and unlimited other vegetables
- Pan-fried Chicken in White Wine (see recipe, page 161) served with 115g (4oz) boiled new potatoes (with skins) and unlimited green vegetables
- Chicken stuffed with Mozzarella and Basil (see recipe, page 156) served with 100g (3½oz) boiled new potatoes (with skins) and unlimited other vegetables
- Spicy Chicken Stir-fry (see recipe, page 164) plus 50g (2oz) [uncooked weight] boiled basmati rice and a large mixed salad
- Chicken Tagine with Orange (see recipe, page 163) plus 50g (2oz) [uncooked weight] boiled basmati rice and a large mixed salad; 1 piece fruit

FISH AND SEAFOOD DINNERS

- 225g (8oz) any white fish, grilled, steamed or microwaved, served with 115g (4oz) boiled new potatoes (with skins) and unlimited other vegetables plus parsley sauce made with skimmed milk; 1 × 110g Rosemary Conley Low Fat Belgian Chocolate Mousse

- 1 × 175g (6oz) salmon steak, grilled and served with 115g (4oz) boiled new potatoes (with skins) and unlimited other vegetables

- Baked Smoked Haddock with Spinach, Tomato and Ginger (see recipe, page 172) plus 115g (4oz) [cooked weight] boiled pasta and unlimited vegetables; Chocolate Orange Cups (see recipe, page 235)

- Smoked Haddock Pasta (see recipe, page 175) served with a mixed salad tossed in Balsamic Dressing (see recipe, page 225); 1 piece fruit

- Steamed Sea Bass with Chilli (see recipe, page 176) served with 150g (5oz) boiled new potatoes (with skins) and unlimited other vegetables; Baked Banana (see recipe, page 241)

- Pan-fried Sole with Lemon, Spinach and Tomato Pesto (see recipe, page 178) served with 100g (3½oz) boiled new potatoes and unlimited other vegetables

- Griddled Swordfish with Horseradish Cream (see recipe, page 238) served with 150g (5oz) new potatoes (with skins) and unlimited other vegetables; 1 piece fruit

- Thai Prawn Rice (see recipe, page 185)

- Prawn Risotto (see recipe, page 182); 1 low-fat yogurt (max. 120 kcal)

VEGETARIAN

- Ⓥ Thai veggie curry: cook chopped spring onions, sliced aubergine, peppers, mange-tout, broccoli florets and thin green beans in a non-stick pan with a little spray oil. Add 1 tsp green curry paste and 150ml (¼ pint) low-fat coconut milk and heat through. Serve with fresh coriander and 75g (3oz) [cooked weight] boiled egg noodles; 1 low-fat yogurt (max. 100 kcal)

- Ⓥ Vegetable fajitas made with chargrilled sliced peppers and red onions wrapped in 1 tortilla and topped with 1 tbsp very low-fat natural fromage frais and 1 tbsp low-fat guacamole. Serve with unlimited salad with fat-free dressing and a little salsa

- Ⓥ 2 Quorn Pork Style Ribsters served with 115g (4oz) boiled new potatoes (with skins) and unlimited green vegetables and grilled tomatoes; 1 × 110g Rosemary Conley Low Fat Belgian Chocolate Mousse

- Ⓥ 1 vegetarian burger, 4 grilled tomatoes, 115g (4oz) mushrooms, grilled, 115g (4oz) peas, and 175g (6oz) boiled new potatoes (with skins). Serve with sauce or pickle of your choice; 1 low-fat yogurt (max. 60 kcal)

- Ⓥ 4 Quorn sausages served with 115g (4oz) boiled new potatoes (with skins), 115g (4oz) peas and unlimited grilled tomatoes; 2 pieces fruit

- Ⓥ Quorn Red Thai Curry (see recipe, page 213) plus 50g (2oz) [uncooked weight] boiled basmati rice; 1 low-fat yogurt (max. 125 kcal)

- Ⓥ Butternut Squash Lasagne (see recipe, page 210) served with a large mixed salad; 1 kiwi fruit

- Ⓥ Lentil Roast (see recipe, page 207) served with Sautéed Courgettes and Cherry Tomatoes (see recipe, page 223); 1 low-fat yogurt (max. 100 kcal)
- Ⓥ Vegetable Chilli (see recipe, page 215) served with 50g (2oz) [uncooked weight] boiled basmati rice and a mixed salad; Cosmopolitan Cocktail (see recipe, page 238)
- Ⓥ Roast Vegetable and Tomato Pasta (see recipe, page 205) served with a small green salad; Fresh Lime Cheesecake (see recipe, page 239)
- Ⓥ Vegetable Rice Bake (see recipe, page 198) served with a large mixed salad; Apricot and Cherry Filo Stack (see recipe, page 237)
- Ⓥ Bean and Burgundy Casserole (see recipe, page 196) served with 100g (3½oz) boiled new potatoes (with skins) and unlimited other vegetables
- Ⓥ Aubergine and Chickpea Curry (see recipe, page 212) served with Citrus Rice Pilaff (see recipe, page 199) and a small green salad; 225g (8oz) fresh fruit salad
- Ⓥ Spicy Chickpea Casserole (see recipe, page 204) served with Crunchy Green Gi Salad (see recipe, page 119); Rhubarb and Apple Fool (see recipe, page 230)
- Ⓥ Sweet and Sour Vegetable Tofu (see recipe, page 214) plus 50g (2oz) [uncooked weight] boiled basmati rice and a large salad
- Ⓥ Crunchy Vegetable Pasta (see recipe, page 201) served with a large salad; Baked Egg Custard (see recipe, page 241)

Power snacks

Approx. 50 kcal each. Select 2 per day

The following Power Snacks have been chosen because of their low Gi and GL rating. They will give you slow-releasing energy food that will help sustain your blood sugar levels until your next meal. Eat one mid-morning and one mid-afternoon.

FRESH FRUIT POWER SNACKS

- 2 kiwi fruits
- 1 small or ½ large banana
- 1 medium pear
- 1 medium peach
- 1 medium apple
- 1 medium nectarine
- 1 medium orange
- 1 whole papaya
- 2 satsumas
- 2 fresh figs
- 2 clementines
- 3 plums
- 4 apricots
- 100g (3½oz) pineapple
- 75g (3oz) seedless grapes
- 100g (3½oz) mango
- 100g (3½oz) cherries
- 1 whole grapefruit
- 150g (5oz) strawberries or raspberries plus 1 tsp 0% fat Greek-style yogurt

DRIED FRUIT POWER SNACKS

- 2 apricots
- 1 fig
- 20g (¾oz) sultanas

VEGETABLE POWER SNACKS

- 8 cherry tomatoes
- 150g (5oz) mixed salad with 1 tsp fat-free dressing
- 8 carrot sticks with 25g (1oz) salsa
- 3 celery sticks with 25g (1oz) low-fat cottage cheese mixed with black pepper and chopped red onion
- 200g (7oz) mixed salad
- 200g (7oz) Crunchy Green Gi Salad (see recipe, page 119)

OTHER POWER SNACKS

- 1 Ryvita Dark Rye crispbread spread with 15g (½oz) low-fat humous
- 15g (½oz) toasted muesli served with milk from allowance and a little low-calorie sugar substitute
- ½ × 35g Rosemary Conley Low Gi Nutrition Bar

Treats

100 kcal each. Select one per day

You can choose any food or drink you like for your 100-calorie treat, and it can fall outside the low-fat, low-Gi guidelines. You can also save up your treats for a special occasion. Remember, it is your choice and your treat. Here are some suggestions.

100-calorie treats with more than 5% fat

HEALTHY AND HIGH FAT TREATS

- 25g (1oz) Brazil nuts
- 15g (½oz) pinenuts
- 25g (1oz) mixed nuts and raisins
- 100g (3½oz) olives (weighed with stones)
- 2 tsps extra virgin olive oil
- 25g (1oz) mozzarella cheese
- 3 tbsps Total Original Greek yogurt
- ½ avocado with 1 tsp low-calorie dressing
- 15g (½oz) butter (including peanut butter)

NAUGHTY BUT NICE TREATS

- 1 × 22g Cadbury's Flake Cake Bar
- 1 × 340g serving Pret A Manger Chocolate Cappuccino
- 1 mini Aero
- 1 treat-size Cadbury's Fudge
- 1 Cadbury's Time Out Orange Finger
- 1 fun-size Milky Way
- 3 After Eight mints
- 2 slices Terry's Chocolate Orange
- 1 Nestlé 2 finger orange Kit Kat

100-calorie treats with 5% or less fat

LOVELY AND LOW FAT TREATS

- 1 M&S Count on Us Lemon Cereal Bar
- 1 M&S Count on Us Tantalising Toffee iced dessert
- 1 meringue nest with 50g (2oz) Yeo Valley Organic Raspberry Yogurt
- 1 Sainsbury's Be Good to Yourself Carrot Cake Slice
- 1 Tesco Healthy Living Carrot and Orange Cake Slice
- 1 × 35g Rosemary Conley Low Gi Nutrition Bar
- 1 Asda Less than 5% fat Cherry Bakewell Slice
- 10 Creamy Lemon Crispy Snack-a-Jacks
- 1 × 25g pack M&S Count on Us Mediterranean Baked Potato Crisps
- 1 × 20g pack M&S Count on Us Bacon Rashers snacks
- 1 × 24g pack Boots Shapers New York Style Salted Pretzels
- 1 × 25g pack Jacob's Thai Bites, any flavour

LIQUID AND LIGHT TREATS

- 1 Cadbury's High Lights chocolate drink
- 1 × 150ml (5fl oz) glass red or dry white wine or champagne
- 1 double pub measure gin or vodka and slimline tonic
- 1 double pub measure rum and Diet Coke
- 1 double pub measure whisky or cognac
- 300ml (½ pint) beer, lager or dry cider

DELICIOUS DESSERT TREATS

- Strawberry brûlée: place 100g (3½oz) strawberries in the bottom of a ramekin dish. Top with 85g (3oz) Total 0% fat Greek-style yogurt and 2 tsps demerara sugar. Place under a preheated hot grill until the sugar caramelises
- Moroccan Clementines (see recipe, page 232) plus 2 tbsps virtually fat free fromage frais
- Strawberries with Black Pepper and Balsamic Dressing (see recipe, page 232)
- 115g (4oz) fresh or frozen raspberries served with 1 low-fat raspberry-flavoured yogurt (max. 75 kcal)
- 1 meringue nest filled with 25g (1oz) any fruit and topped with 1 tbsp low-fat fromage frais
- Strawberry Dream (see recipe, page 233)
- Cardamom and Orange Rice Pudding (see recipe, page 234) served with 2 tbsps virtually fat free fromage frais
- Chocolate Orange Cups (see recipe, page 235)
- Rhubarb and Apple Fool (see recipe, page 230)
- Cranberry and Orange Granita Sorbet (see recipe, page 236)
- Baked Banana (see recipe, page 241)
- Baked Stuffed Apple (see recipe, page 240)
- Baked Egg Custard (see recipe, page 241)
- Cosmopolitan Cocktail (see recipe, page 238) served with 2 tbsps virtually fat free fromage frais
- Blackberry and Port Ice (see recipe, page 231)
- 1 × 110g Rosemary Conley Belgian Chocolate Mousse

Busy day menu plan

On those days when you don't have time to prepare elaborate meals, there are plenty of quick and easy options in the Gi Jeans Diet menu plans that will suit. Many of the lunch suggestions are also ideal for a packed lunch.

So, a typical busy day's menu plan could look like this:

Daily Allowance
450ml (¾ pint) semi-skimmed milk

Breakfast
40g (1½oz) muesli served with milk from allowance and 1 tsp brown sugar

Power Snack (11 am)
1 small banana

Lunch
2 slices multigrain bread spread with 2 tsps horseradish sauce and topped with 50g (2oz) pastrami and 4 cherry tomatoes; 1 apple
OR
1 low-fat prepacked sandwich (made with multigrain bread) or salad (max. 300 kcal)

Power Snack (3.30pm)
2 clementines

Dinner

175g (6oz) chicken pieces dry-fried with chopped onion, peppers, mushrooms, courgettes and sweetcorn plus ½ can low-fat wine cook-in-sauce. Serve with 50g (2oz) [uncooked weight] boiled basmati rice; 1 low-fat yogurt or fromage frais (max. 100 kcal)

OR

Any low-fat pasta ready meal (max. 450 kcal) served with a mixed salad and 1 tsp fat-free dressing

Treat

1 Nestlé 2 finger orange Kit Kat

Alcohol

1 small glass red wine

11 The No Diet Gi Jeans Diet

If you want to lose weight and eat a healthier diet but you really don't want to follow a diet plan, then just follow these simple rules. You will lose weight, but you may not lose it as fast as you would on the main Gi Jeans Diet.

Dos

1 **DO** eat three moderate-sized meals a day – a breakfast, lunch and dinner. Form your meal selections around the foods in the GREEN and AMBER lists in the Traffic Light guide (see pages 100–3).

2 **DO** limit your alcohol consumption to one unit of alcohol per day for women, two for men.

3 **DO** look at the nutrition labels on every item of food before you buy it. Only purchase those products that contain 5% or less fat.

4 **DO** cut out all visible fat from your diet – that includes all butter, margarines, polyunsaturated low-fat spreads, oil (including olive oil), lard, dripping, cream, crème fraîche, French dressing, mayonnaise, and so on.

5 **DO** select low- or medium-Gi foods that are high in fibre.

6 **DO** eat at least five fruit and/or vegetable portions a day.

7 **DO** eat enough at meal times to fill you up so that you are not tempted to snack on high-fat foods between meals. Vegetables are great fillers with your main meal. Aim to fill half your plate with vegetables or salad, a quarter with pasta, rice or new potatoes and a quarter with protein food (e.g. meat, poultry, fish, Quorn).

8 **DO** drink 450ml (¾ pint) semi-skimmed or skimmed milk each day – in tea, coffee and on breakfast cereals.

9 **DO** drink as much water as possible, and low-calorie drinks are unrestricted.

10 **DO** dine out with care. Avoid anything fried, coated in breadcrumbs or batter or cooked in pastry. Choose new potatoes in preference to chips. Select pasta dishes in tomato-based sauces rather than creamy ones. Ask for your food to be cooked without fat and have fat-free dressings on salads.

11 **DO** choose soup as a starter – it is a good filler. Choose consommé or vegetable-based soups rather than creamy ones, but do without the bread roll.

12 **DO** balance the effects of a sumptuous meal out with extra exercise the next day.

13 **DO** take every opportunity to increase your activity levels. Use the stairs more, and walk further and more often.

14 **DO** try to do 30 minutes of aerobic activity on five days a week.

Don'ts

1 **DON'T** eat just one massive meal a day.

2 **DON'T** skip meals.

3 **DON'T** nibble anything other than one piece of fruit or some chopped raw vegetables between meals.
4 **DON'T** eat any chocolate or sweets.
5 **DON'T** eat biscuits, cakes, pastries or anything with more than 5% fat content except for oily fish.
6 **DON'T** eat any of the foods from the RED list in the Traffic Light guide (see page 102–3).

If you stick to these guidelines, you will lose weight and inches. If you cheat, you may not and you may be better suited to the more formal Gi Jeans Diet eating plan, which includes treats. It is also important that you follow the exercise recommendations in chapter 6.

Traffic light guide to foods

GREEN

These foods form the basis of the No Diet Gi Jeans Diet.

- Beans and pulses (including baked beans)
- Bread: multigrain or stoneground; pitta bread; tortilla wraps
- Cereals: whole-oat or high-fibre brands; muesli; porridge oats; Weetabix; Special K; Shredded Wheat
- Cheese: brands with 5% or less fat, e.g. cottage cheese
- Fish: white fish grilled, steamed or microwaved; fresh or canned tuna; oily fish such as salmon, mackerel, sardines (max. 2 × 50g/2oz servings per week)
- Fromage frais: brands with 5% or less fat
- Fruit: fresh, dried, frozen or canned in natural juice (except ackee, coconut, olives)
- Fruit juice
- Herbs and spices: choose fresh ones where possible

- Meat: lean cuts of beef, pork, lamb, with all visible fat removed and grilled, dry-fried or roasted; extra-lean mince
- Milk: skimmed or semi-skimmed, cow's, goat's or soya
- Nuts: chestnuts
- Oats (including porridge oats)
- Pasta and noodles: boiled and served without fat
- Potatoes: sweet potatoes, boiled or dry-roasted; new potatoes, boiled or dry-roasted; old potatoes boiled, baked or dry-roasted, ideally combined with low-Gi food such as baked beans or pulses
- Poultry: lean chicken and turkey without skin, grilled, dry-fried or roasted; turkey rashers grilled or dry-fried
- Quorn: cooked without fat
- Rice: basmati or brown long-grain, boiled or steamed
- Salad items: salad leaves, tomatoes, cucumber, cress, raw mushrooms, celery, peppers, courgettes, onions
- Sauces: brands with 5% or less fat
- Soups: brands with 5% or less fat
- Soya and soya products: with 5% or less fat
- Tea and coffee: drunk black or with milk from allowance
- Vegetables (except avocado)
- Water
- Yogurt: brands with 5% or less fat; 0% fat Greek-style yogurt

AMBER

The following foods may be consumed in moderation on the No Diet Gi Jeans Diet.

- Alcohol: 1 unit per day for women, 2 for men
- Cereal bars: brands with 5% or less fat
- Cheese: reduced-fat

- Condiments
- Cooking oil sprays: low-fat brands
- Crispbreads: high-fibre brands with 5% or less fat
- Dressings: brands with 5% or less fat
- Gravy: made with gravy powder or low-fat granules
- Honey: if combined with low-Gi food such as porridge
- Jams and preserves (except lemon curd): if combined with low-Gi food such as multigrain bread
- Eggs (max. 3 a week)
- Meat: low-fat sausages grilled, lean bacon grilled
- Pastry: filo
- Pickles and relishes
- Stock cubes: vegetable, meat and chicken
- Yorkshire pudding: made with skimmed milk and cooked in a non-stick pan

RED

Avoid these foods while following the No Diet Gi Jeans Diet.

- Biscuits and cakes
- Black pudding
- Bread: ordinary white and brown bread except multigrain or stoneground varieties
- Butter (including peanut butter)
- Butterscotch
- Cereal bars: brands with more than 5% fat
- Cheese: all varieties except cottage cheese or brands with 5% or less fat
- Chocolates/chocolate spread
- Cocoa and cocoa products (including drinking chocolate)
- Crackers: with more than 5% fat

- Cream and soured cream
- Cream from full-fat milk
- Crème fraîche
- Crème caramel
- Crisps (including low-fat crisps and snacks)
- Dressings and sauces: brands with more than 5% fat
- Dripping
- Egg custard
- Fudge
- Fatty meats
- Fromage frais: brands with more than 5% fat
- Fried foods (except dry-fried)
- Horlicks
- Lard
- Lemon curd
- Margarines and spreads (including low-fat spreads)
- Mayonnaise
- Marzipan
- Meat products: Cornish pasties, faggots, haggis, pâté, pork pies, salami, scotch eggs; sausages with more than 5% fat
- Nuts (except chestnuts)
- Oil (including olive oil)
- Olives
- Pastry
- Puddings: made with butter or cream; sponge puddings
- Quiches
- Rice (except basmati or brown long-grain rice)
- Suet
- Yogurt: brands with more than 5% fat

12 Cooking the low–fat way

Cooking low fat is easier than you think. It just takes a little bit of imagination. There are many low-fat foods that can be substituted for the high-fat ones you are probably used to including in your culinary exploits. In the next few pages I will explain the benefits of using the appropriate implements and utensils and explain how you can change your cooking techniques to enable you to make low-fat recipes that taste delicious. It will not take you long to automatically refrain from using oil and discover that cooking with wine, garlic and herbs can still leave your tastebuds dancing.

Equipment you will need

Investing in good, solid, hard-wearing equipment will certainly be worthwhile as you find how easy it is to cook the low-fat way. A top-quality, non-stick wok or frying pan is ideal for stir-frying and dry-frying. Try to buy one with a lid if possible, as this helps keep in the moisture and aids thorough cooking of meat and poultry. I have a non-stick electric wok which has revolutionised my cooking!

Non-stick saucepans are useful for cooking sauces, porridge, scrambled eggs and other foods that tend to stick easily. Always use non-stick utensils with your non-stick pans. Also, treat yourself to a set of non-stick baking tins and trays. Cakes, Yorkshire puddings, scones and lots more dishes can all be cooked the low-fat way.

Choosing the right pan

There are many factors to take into account when selecting pans. Weight, ease of handling and cost are but a few. Heavy-based pans are the most efficient conductors of heat and ensure a constant quick heat to the food. This style of pan, coupled with a non-stick surface, is definitely the best choice. Always select the correct-sized pan for the job. Cooking a small quantity in a large pan will cause the pan to burn in areas where the food has no contact. Conversely, too much food in a small pan will result in the food cooking unevenly.

When cleaning non-stick pans, always soak the pans first to loosen any food still inside (stubborn stains should be soaked overnight). Then wash in hot soapy water, preferably with a sponge or soft cloth or custom-made pad for cleaning non-stick pans. Never use abrasive cleaning materials or abrasive pads, as these will scratch and destroy the non-stick surface.

Non-scratch utensils

Wooden spoons and spatulas, Teflon-coated tools and others marked as suitable for use with non-stick surfaces are a must. If you continue to use metal forks, spoons and spatulas, you will scratch and spoil the non-stick surface. Treat the surfaces kindly and good non-stick pans will last for years.

Store cupboard

There are many staple ingredients that are very useful to have in stock. Build up your store cupboard over a period of time.

STOCK ITEMS
- Arrowroot
- Artificial sweetener
- Bovril
- Cooking spray oil
- Dried herbs
- Dressings: fat-free salad dressing, reduced-oil salad dressing
- Vinegar: balsamic vinegar; white wine vinegar
- Flour: cornflour, plain flour, self-raising flour, stoneground flour
- Gelatine or Vege Gel
- Lemon juice
- Marmite
- Oats
- Pasta (various shapes and types)
- Peppercorns: black or green peppercorns, white pepper
- Rice: basmati or long-grain brown
- Salt
- Sauces: tomato ketchup, HP fruity sauce, barbecue sauce, soy sauce, Tabasco sauce, Worcestershire sauce
- Stock cubes: vegetable, chicken, beef, lamb, pork
- Sugar: caster sugar, demerara sugar, low-calorie sugar substitute such as Silver Spoon's Half Spoon

FRESH ITEMS

- Eggs
- Garlic
- Ginger
- Fresh herbs
- Lemons
- Oranges
- Tomatoes

Basic cooking techniques

When cooking and preparing low-fat dishes it's important to add moisture and extra flavour to compensate for the lack of oil or fat. Wine, water, soy sauce, wine vinegar, and even fresh lemon juice all provide liquid in which food can be 'fried' or cooked. Some thicker types of sauces can dry out too fast if they are added early on in cooking, so add them later when there is more moisture in the pan.

How to dry-fry foods

One of the key methods used in low-fat cooking is dry-frying, which does away with the need to use oil. The trick is to have your non-stick pan over the correct heat. If it's much too hot, the pan will dry out too soon and the contents will burn. If the heat is too low, you lose the crispness recommended for a stir-fry. Practice makes perfect and a simple rule is to preheat the empty pan until it is hot (but not too hot) before adding any of the ingredients. Test if the pan is hot enough by adding a piece of meat or poultry. The pan is at the right temperature if the meat sizzles on contact. Once the meat or poultry is sealed on all sides (when it changes colour) you can reduce the heat a little as you add any other ingredients.

Cooking meat and poultry is simple, as the natural fat and juices run out almost immediately, providing plenty of moisture to prevent burning. When cooking minced meat it's best to dry-fry it first and then place the meat in a colander to drain away any fat that has emerged. Wipe out the pan with a wad of kitchen paper to remove any fatty residue before continuing to cook your shepherd's pie or bolognese sauce, or whatever. If you are using onions, always add them after you have dry-fried the meat and wiped out the pan or they will soak up the fat from the meat like a sponge.

Vegetables contain their own juices and soon release them when they become hot, so dry-frying vegetables works well too. When dry-frying vegetables it is important not to overcook them. They should be crisp and colourful so that they retain their flavour and most of their nutrients. Perhaps the most impressive results are obtained with onions. After a few minutes they go from being raw to translucent and soft and then on to become brown and caramelised.

Good results are also obtained when dry-frying large quantities of mushrooms, as they sweat and make lots of liquid. Using just a few mushrooms produces a less satisfactory result unless you are stir-frying them with lots of other vegetables. If you are using just a small quantity, therefore, you may find it preferable to cook them in vegetable stock.

Occasionally you may wish to add a little cooking spray oil to line your pan or baking tin to aid the cooking or baking of dishes such as 'fried' eggs, fish, cakes, Yorkshire puddings, and so on. Make sure you choose a low-calorie one and use sparingly.

Flavour enhancers

Herbs can be added to virtually any dish to enhance its flavour. Dried herbs are more strongly flavoured than fresh, although it's best to use fresh herbs where possible as some nutrients are lost during the drying process. As a general rule, 1 tsp of dried herbs equals 4 tsps of fresh.

There are many varieties of blended spice mixes to add heat and flavour to all kinds of meat and vegetable dishes. These are great for a quick and easy curry sauce, although many of the individual spice flavours are lost during the blending. Using one or two spices to flavour food rather than a blend adds a more distinctive delicate flavour. As spices need to be cooked out in order to obtain the maximum favour, always start by dry-frying spices in a wok or infusing the spice in the cooking liquor for 2–3 minutes before adding the main ingredient.

Adding freshly ground black pepper to just about any savoury dish is a real flavour enhancer. You need a good pepper mill and, ideally, you should buy your peppercorns whole and in large quantities. Ready-ground black pepper is nowhere near as good.

When cooking rice, pasta and vegetables, add a vegetable stock cube to the cooking water. Although stock cubes do contain some fat, the amount absorbed by the food is negligible and the benefit in flavour is noticeable. Always save the cooking water from vegetables to make soups, gravy and sauces. Again, the fat from the stock cube, divided between however many portions you are serving is very small.

Here is a quick reference list of ingredients that can be substituted for traditional high-fat ones:

Cheese sauces Use small amounts of low-fat Cheddar, a little made-up mustard and skimmed milk with cornflour.

Custard Use custard powder and follow the instructions on the packet, using skimmed milk and artificial sweetener in place of sugar to save more calories.

Cream Instead of double cream or whipping cream, use 0% fat Greek yogurt or fromage frais. Do not boil. Instead of single cream, use natural or vanilla-flavoured yogurt or fromage frais.

Cream cheese Use Quark (low-fat skimmed soft cheese).

Creamed potatoes Mash potatoes in the usual way and add fromage frais in place of butter or cream. Season well. Use new potatoes in preference to old ones to keep the Gi rating low.

Roux Make a low-fat roux by adding dry plain flour to a pan containing the other ingredients and 'cooking out' the flour, then add liquid to thicken. Alternatively, use cornflour mixed with cold water or milk, bring to the boil and cook for around 2–3 minutes.

Thickening for sweet sauces Arrowroot, slaked in cold water or juice, is good because it becomes translucent when cooked.

Stocks

Any chef will tell you that the secret of a good sauce relies on a very good stock. Home-made stock is well worth the effort, as the final flavours are quite different from any convenient stock cube alternatives. If you do decide to make your own stock, make sure you chill it completely. This allows the fat to set, making it easy to remove and discard before adding the stock to your cooking.

There are four basic stocks which are used as a base for many dishes. White stock is pale and light and made from meat and poultry. Unbrowned beef and chicken are excellent for this purpose, while lamb, pork and duck contain much higher levels of fat. Brown stock is made by browning the meat or bones first – you can either dry-fry the meat in a non-stick pan or roast in a hot oven (the latter method gives a darker colour). Both white and brown stock are then flavoured with root vegetables such as carrots, celery, onions and leeks and left to simmer in plenty of water for 1½–2 hours. A brown stock may be coloured with tomato purée or gravy browning for a deep finish.

Fish stock is quite different and needs careful cooking. The stock should not be allowed to simmer for more than 20 minutes or the bones will make the stock bitter. You can use the bones, heads, skin and tails of any white fish such as sole, brill or plaice. Avoid fatty fish such as mackerel, which will make the stock oily.

Vegetable stock can be made easily by simmering a wide selection of fresh vegetables, taking care not to overpower the flavour with one particular ingredient. You can add tomato puree for additional flavour.

Many recipes in this book use stock cubes for convenience and it is well worth spending a little extra on the better quality ones. Generally, one stock cube will make up with 600ml (1 pint) of water.

Salad dressings

The secret of a good salad is in the dressing. The key is to learn how to make a good dressing without using oil, and it really isn't that difficult. Try it, and you'll be amazed how quickly your tastebuds adapt. Once you've followed a low-fat diet for any length of time, you'll find the taste of oil becomes extremely unpalatable.

As acidic foods lower the Gi content of a meal, try sprinkling vinegar or lemon juice on your salads. Here are some further ideas for low-fat or fat-free dressings:

- Balsamic Dressing (see recipe, page 225).
- Fat-free Mayonnaise (see recipe, page 225).
- Honey and Orange Dressing (see recipe, page 226).
- Oil-free Vinaigrette (see recipe, page 227).
- Garlic and Yogurt Dressing (see recipe, page 228).
- Marie Rose Dressing (see recipe, page 228).
- Oil-free Orange and Lemon Vinaigrette (see recipe, page 229).

13 Recipes

Ⓥ means suitable for vegetarians

❄ means suitable for home freezing

Soups

Black bean soup

SERVES 6
1 SERVING 312 KCAL/2G FAT
PREPARATION TIME 15 MINUTES
COOKING TIME 1 HOUR 15 MINUTES

The beans need to be soaked overnight and rinsed thoroughly before use.

450g (1lb) black beans, soaked overnight
2 onions, finely sliced
2 garlic cloves, chopped
2 large carrots, diced
3 young celery sticks, diced
1 tsp smoked paprika
4 sage leaves
1.2 litres (2 pints) vegetable stock
½ wine glass white wine
2 tbsps virtually fat free fromage frais

1 Place all the ingredients except the white wine and fromage frais in a large saucepan and bring to the boil. Reduce the heat and simmer for 1 hour until the beans are tender, adding more liquid if required.
2 Allow the soup to cool, then transfer to a food processor and blend until smooth.
3 Return the soup to the pan and add the white wine. Reheat the soup and serve hot with a swirl of virtually fat free fromage frais.

Gingered carrot soup ⓥ ❋

SERVES 4
1 SERVING 106 KCAL/1.9G FAT
PREPARATION TIME 20 MINUTES
COOKING TIME 30 MINUTES

1kg (2lb) fresh young carrots, sliced
3 celery sticks, sliced
2 medium onions, chopped
1 garlic clove, crushed
25g (1oz) fresh ginger, peeled and chopped
few sprigs of chopped fresh thyme
1.2 litres (2 pints) vegetable stock
2 bay leaves
salt and freshly ground black pepper
chopped fresh chives to garnish

1 Place the carrots, celery, onions and garlic in a large
  saucepan and dry-fry over a low heat for 2–3 minutes.
2 Add the ginger, thyme, stock and bay leaves and simmer
  gently until the vegetables are soft. Remove the bay and
  transfer the soup to a liquidiser or blender and liquidise until
  smooth. Adjust the consistency with a little extra stock, if
  required, and season with salt and black pepper.
3 Garnish with chopped fresh chives and serve hot or cold.

Cauliflower and stilton soup ⓥ ❄

SERVES 4
1 SERVING 216 KCAL/12G FAT
PREPARATION TIME 10 MINUTES
COOKING TIME 30 MINUTES

1 large cauliflower
2 medium onions, chopped
1 garlic clove, crushed
600ml (1 pint) vegetable stock
½ tsp English mustard powder
2 bay leaves
300ml (½ pint) skimmed milk
115g (4oz) Stilton cheese
salt and freshly ground black pepper
2 tbsps chopped fresh flat leaf parsley to garnish

1 Remove and discard the outer leaves from the cauliflower
   and coarsely chop the rest, including the stalk. Place in a
   large saucepan. Add the onions, garlic, vegetable stock,
   mustard powder, and bay leaves.
2 Bring to the boil then reduce the heat and simmer gently for
   15–20 minutes until the vegetables are soft. Allow to cool
   slightly, then liquidise in batches in a liquidiser or food
   processor, adding a little of the milk and Stilton to each
   batch until smooth and lump free.
3 Return the soup to the pan and season with salt and black
   pepper. Adjust the consistency with a little extra milk if
   required. Garnish with finely chopped parsley and serve
   immediately.

Thyme-flavoured white bean soup

SERVES 2
1 SERVING 134 KCAL/4.4G FAT
SOAKING TIME OVERNIGHT
PREPARATION TIME 15 MINUTES
COOKING TIME 60 MINUTES

50g (2oz) white beans (cannelloni or haricot), soaked overnight
4 rashers smoked lean back bacon, cut into strips (optional)
4 small shallots, finely chopped
2 garlic cloves, crushed
2 celery sticks, chopped
2 tsps chopped fresh thyme
2–3 tsps vegetable stock bouillon powder
150ml (¼ pint) skimmed milk
freshly ground black pepper

1 Rinse the beans well, place in a large saucepan, cover with
   water and bring to the boil. Simmer gently for 30 minutes.
2 In a separate non-stick pan dry-fry the bacon (if using),
   shallots, garlic and celery for 5–6 minutes until soft. Place in
   the saucepan with the beans, and add the thyme and
   bouillon powder. Reduce the heat and simmer gently for 30
   minutes, topping up with water as required.
3 After 30 minutes the beans should be soft. Ladle the soup
   into a food processor and blend until smooth. Return to the
   heat and adjust the consistency with a little skimmed milk.
   Season well with black pepper and serve hot.

Creamy red lentil soup ⓥ

SERVES 4
1 SERVING 204 KCAL/1.3G FAT
PREPARATION TIME 20 MINUTES
COOKING TIME 25 MINUTES

1 onion, chopped
1 garlic clove, crushed
2 celery stalks, chopped
2 carrots, chopped
2 tsps chopped fresh thyme
1 tsp ground cumin
175g (6oz) dried red lentils
1.2 litres (2 pints) vegetable stock
1 × 400g can chopped tomatoes
freshly ground black pepper
2 tbsps virtually fat free fromage frais
1 tbsp chopped fresh parsley to garnish

1 In a large non-stick saucepan dry-fry the onion until soft.
   Add the remaining ingredients except the fromage frais and
   parsley and bring to the boil. Reduce the heat and simmer
   gently for 20 minutes until the lentils are soft.
2 Allow to cool slightly then blend with a stick blender, or
   purée in small batches in a food processor. Thin the soup
   down with a little extra vegetable stock or water. Reheat in a
   saucepan as required.
3 Just before serving, remove from the heat, stir in the
   fromage frais and season to taste with black pepper. Spoon
   into bowls and garnish with chopped parsley.

Salads

Crunchy green Gi salad Ⓥ

SERVES 1
1 SERVING 45 KCAL/0.09G FAT (EXCLUDING DRESSING)
PREPARATION TIME 15 MINUTES

50g (2oz) salad leaves of your choice, shredded
½ green pepper, seeded and chopped
1 × 2.5cm (1in) chunk cucumber, chopped
4 spring onions, chopped
2 celery sticks, trimmed and finely chopped
4 basil leaves left whole (optional)
5 fresh mange-tout or sugar snap peas, coarsely chopped

1 Place all the ingredients in a bowl and mix well.
2 Add Oil-free Vinaigrette (see recipe, page 227) to taste and
   toss well.

Prawn and pasta salad

SERVES 4
1 SERVING 255 KCAL/2.2G FAT
PREPARATION TIME 15 MINUTES

450g (1lb) [cooked weight] pasta shells
450g (1lb) cooked shelled prawns
150g (5oz) low-fat natural yogurt
1 tbsp tomato purée
a few drops Tabasco sauce to taste (optional)
3 spring onions, chopped

1 Combine the cooked pasta shells and prawns in a serving bowl.
2 Combine the yogurt, tomato purée and Tabasco sauce, then pour onto the pasta mixture and toss well.
3 Just before serving, sprinkle with the chopped spring onions. Serve with a green salad.

Courgette and red onion salad ⓥ

SERVES 4
1 SERVING 56 KCAL/0.5G FAT
PREPARATION TIME 15 MINUTES
COOKING TIME 5 MINUTES

225g (8oz) baby courgettes
2 large red onions, finely sliced
pinch of crushed green peppercorns
salt
½ tsp coriander seed
2 fresh sage leaves
2 tbsps fruit vinegar
2 tbsps chopped fresh parsley
salad leaves to serve

1 Using a chopping knife, cut the courgettes into 2.5cm (1in) batons.
2 Preheat a non-stick frying pan or wok. Add the courgettes, onions, coriander seed, sage and a little salt and dry-fry until browned.
3 Arrange the salad leaves on a serving dish. Add the vegetables. Drizzle with fruit vinegar and garnish with chopped parsley.

Chicken couscous salad

SERVES 4
1 SERVING 326 KCAL/4.8G FAT
PREPARATION TIME 20 MINUTES
COOKING TIME 5 MINUTES

4 skinless chicken breasts, sliced into strips
1 garlic clove, crushed
1 tsp ground coriander
¼ tsp ground turmeric
1 vegetable stock cube, dissolved in 400ml (14fl oz)
    boiling water
170g (6oz) couscous
1 tbsp finely chopped chives
1 tbsp chopped fresh basil
4 tomatoes, skinned, seeded and diced
½ cucumber, peeled and diced
freshly ground black pepper
fresh basil and fresh orange wedges to garnish

for the dressing
150ml (¼ pint) fresh orange juice
2 tsps chopped fresh ginger
1 tbsp good quality white wine vinegar
1 tsp Dijon mustard

1 Mix together the dressing ingredients in a large bowl. Add
   the chicken and toss in the dressing. Season well with black
   pepper.
2 Preheat a non-stick wok or deep non-stick saucepan. Using
   a slotted spoon, lift the chicken from the dressing, place in
   the pan and dry-fry for 8–10 minutes until completely sealed

and cooked. Add the garlic, coriander and turmeric and cook for a further 2 minutes.

3 Add the stock and dressing and bring to the boil. Gradually add the couscous, stirring well. Cover with a lid, remove from the heat and allow to stand for 1 minute. Remove the lid and, using 2 forks, fluff up the couscous grains.

Cucumber and white bean salad ⓥ

SERVES 4
1 SERVING 136 KCAL/1.2G FAT
PREPARATION TIME 10 MINUTES

1 large cucumber, peeled
1 medium red onion, finely sliced
1 × 400g can cannellini beans, drained and rinsed
1 tsp mustard seed
3 tbsps low-fat natural yogurt
1 garlic clove, crushed
1 tbsp chopped fresh mint
freshly ground black pepper
salad leaves to serve

1 Cut the cucumber in half. Using a vegetable peeler, slice thin strips into a mixing bowl. Add the red onion, beans and mustard seed. Season with black pepper to taste and combine well.

2 In a separate bowl, mix together the yogurt, garlic and mint, adding plenty of black pepper to taste. Pour this dressing over the cucumber and bean mixture and toss well together.

3 Arrange the cucumber and bean salad on a bed of salad leaves and serve immediately.

Potato and watercress salad

SERVES 6
1 SERVING 129 KCAL/2.4G FAT
PREPARATION TIME 30 MINUTES
COOKING TIME 35 MINUTES

450–675g (1–1½lb) new potatoes
1 vegetable stock cube
115g (4oz) lean back bacon
4 spring onions *or* 2 tbsps chopped fresh chives
1 bunch fresh watercress
1 tbsp chopped fresh parsley

for the dressing
150g (5oz) low-fat natural yogurt
2–3 tsps French mustard
1 tsp caster sugar or artificial sweetener to taste
1 tbsp wine vinegar
salt and freshly ground black pepper

1 Scrub the potatoes and cook whole. Cook in boiling water
   with the vegetable stock cube until just tender. Drain well
   and place under cold running water until completely cold.
   Drain well.
2 In the meantime, remove any fat from the bacon and grill the
   rashers until they are crisp. Drain on kitchen paper.
3 Trim and slice the spring onions (if using). Coarsely chop the
   watercress. Place the potatoes in a bowl with the spring
   onions or chives and the watercress. Crush the bacon into
   small pieces and sprinkle into the mixture.

4 Mix together all the ingredients for the dressing and check the seasoning. Pour over the potatoes and mix well. Sprinkle with the chopped parsley, cover and refrigerate until required.

Mixed bean salad with balsamic vinegar and lime ⓥ

SERVES 6
1 SERVING 214 KCAL/1.7G FAT
PREPARATION TIME 20 MINUTES
COOKING TIME 10 MINUTES

1 × 450g can pinto beans
1 × 450g can cannellini beans
225g (8oz) fine green beans, cooked
225g (8oz) baby broad beans, cooked
green lettuce leaves to serve

for the dressing
1 red onion, finely chopped
2 tbsps balsamic vinegar
zest and juice of 1 fresh lime
1 tsp coarse grain mustard
1 tbsp chopped fresh chives

1 Rinse the canned beans and drain well. Mix with the cooked beans.
2 Combine all the dressing ingredients and mix with the beans.
3 Line a serving dish with crisp green lettuce leaves and spoon the salad on top.

Curried chicken and yogurt pasta salad

SERVES 1
1 SERVING 250 KCAL/3G FAT
PREPARATION TIME 10 MINUTES

150g (5oz) natural yogurt
1 tsp curry powder
75g (3oz) cooked chicken breast, cut into cubes
75g (3oz) cooked pasta
unlimited green salad vegetables

1 Mix together the yogurt and curry powder in a bowl.
2 Add the chicken and pasta and stir well.
3 Serve on a bed of fresh green salad vegetables.

Curried chicken and potato salad

SERVES 1
1 SERVING 294 KCAL/3.9G FAT
PREPARATION TIME 5 MINUTES

75g (3oz) cooked chicken breast
115g (4oz) new potatoes, boiled and cut into small pieces
3 tbsps low-fat natural yogurt
1 tbsp low-fat dressing
1 tsp curry powder
1 tsp tomato sauce

1 Cut the chicken into cubes. Mix together the chicken and the
   potatoes.
2 Mix together the remaining ingredients and stir into the
   chicken and potato mix.

Saffron couscous salad Ⓥ

SERVES 4
1 SERVING 122 KCAL/1G FAT
PREPARATION TIME 20 MINUTES
COOKING TIME 5 MINUTES

400ml (14fl oz) vegetable stock
good pinch of saffron
1 tsp ground coriander
1 garlic clove, crushed
175g (6oz) couscous
1 tbsp finely chopped fresh chives
1 tbsp chopped fresh coriander
4 tomatoes, skinned, seeded and diced
½ cucumber, peeled and diced
juice of 1 lemon
salt and freshly ground black pepper
1 tbsp chopped fresh mint to garnish

1 In a large saucepan bring the stock to the boil and add the
   saffron, coriander and garlic.
2 Gradually pour in the couscous, stirring well. Cover with a lid,
   remove from the heat and allow to stand for 1 minute.
3 Remove the lid and, using 2 forks, fluff up the couscous
   grains. Transfer to a large bowl and add the herbs, tomatoes
   and cucumber. Mix well, and season to taste.
4 Pile into a serving dish and drizzle with the lemon juice.
   Garnish with chopped fresh mint.

Coronation chicken

SERVES 4
1 SERVING 287 KCAL/3.2G FAT
PREPARATION TIME 15 MINUTES

4 cooked skinless chicken breasts
225g (8oz) virtually fat free fromage frais
1 tbsp curry powder
2 tbsps mango chutney
225g (8oz) seedless grapes
2 tbsps lemon juice
1 tbsp chopped fresh parsley
salt and freshly ground black pepper
bunch of watercress to serve

1 Coarsely chop the cooked chicken and place in a mixing
   bowl.
2 Blend together the fromage frais, curry powder and mango
   chutney. Mix with the chicken, coating the chicken well.
3 Cut the grapes in half with a sharp knife, add to the chicken
   and combine all the ingredients well. At this point you can
   leave the dish to stand or store it in the refrigerator until
   ready to serve.
4 Just before serving, mix in the lemon juice and the parsley
   and season with salt and pepper.

Chicken Caesar salad

SERVES 4
1 SERVING 138 KCAL/5.8G FAT
PREPARATION TIME 10 MINUTES
COOKING TIME 15 MINUTES

4 boned and skinned chicken breasts
1 romaine or iceberg lettuce
8 spring onions, sliced
½ cucumber, cut into batons

for the dressing
4 tbsps low-fat salad dressing
1 tbsp virtually fat free fromage frais
1 garlic clove, crushed
fresh lemon juice to taste
salt and freshly ground black pepper

1 Preheat a non-stick frying pan. Slice the chicken into strips
   and season well. Place in the pan and cook briskly, turning
   regularly, for 8–10 minutes.
2 Shred the lettuce and place in a large bowl. Add the spring
   onions and cucumber, mix well and arrange on a serving dish.
3 Combine the dressing ingredients in a small bowl. Place the
   cooked chicken on the salad and drizzle the dressing over.

Warm steak and blue cheese salad

SERVES 1
1 SERVING 300 KCAL/8G FAT
PREPARATION TIME 10 MINUTES
COOKING TIME 15 MINUTES

100g (3½oz) new potatoes
mixed salad leaves
2 spring onions
115g (4oz) thin-sliced frying steak
3 tbsps low-fat blue cheese dressing
freshly ground black pepper

1 Cook the new potatoes in boiling water. Drain the potatoes
   and cut into slices.
2 Arrange the salad leaves on a plate. Chop the spring onions
   and scatter over the salad leaves.
3 Dry-fry the steak in a preheated non-stick pan. When
   cooked but still warm, add the steak to the salad along with
   the sliced potatoes. Spoon the dressing on top. Serve
   immediately.

Lemon seafood salad

SERVES 1
1 SERVING 250 KCAL/6G FAT
PREPARATION TIME 15 MINUTES
COOKING TIME 15 MINUTES

100g (3½oz) smoked salmon, cut into ribbons
10 cooked shelled king prawns
salad leaves (rocket, spinach and watercress)

for the dressing
100g (3½oz) 0% fat Greek-style yogurt
1 tsp lemon juice
zest of ½ lemon
2 tsps chopped fresh dill
freshly ground black pepper

1   To make the dressing, mix the yogurt with the lemon juice
    and zest and the chopped dill. Season with freshly ground
    black pepper.
2   Arrange the smoked salmon and prawns over the salad
    leaves. Spoon the dressing over the leaves.

Beef

Braised beef steaks with wild mushrooms

SERVES 4
1 SERVING 375 KCAL/11G FAT
PREPARATION TIME 15 MINUTES
COOKING TIME 40 MINUTES

4 extra lean braising steaks (approx. 175g/6oz each)
2 red onions, finely chopped
2 garlic cloves, crushed
2 tsps chopped fresh thyme
2 beef stock cubes, dissolved in 600ml (1 pint) boiling water
2 tbsps plain flour
1 × 400g can chopped tomatoes
1 wine glass red wine
12 baby carrots, peeled
3 celery sticks, cut into batons
12 button mushrooms
salt and freshly ground black pepper

1 Preheat the oven to 180C, 350F, Gas Mark 4.
2 Season both sides of the beef steaks with salt and black
   pepper, then place in a preheated non-stick pan. Seal on
   both sides until lightly browned, then remove from the pan
   and place in an ovenproof dish.
3 Add the onions, garlic and thyme and cook gently for 2–3
   minutes until soft.

4 Add 2 tbsps of stock then sprinkle the flour over, stir well and cook for 1 minute to 'cook out' the flour.

5 Gradually stir in the remaining stock with the tomatoes and wine. Add the carrots, celery and mushrooms, then pour the sauce over the beef steaks.

6 Cover and place in the oven for 35–40 minutes until the sauce has reduced and the meat is tender.

Beef stroganoff

SERVES 4
1 SERVING 300 KCAL/10.8G FAT
PREPARATION TIME 15 MINUTES
COOKING TIME 20 MINUTES

1 medium onion, finely chopped
2 garlic cloves, crushed
450g (1lb) lean beef fillet, sliced
1 tbsp flour
1 wine glass white wine
150ml (¼ pint) beef stock
1 tbsp Dijon mustard
225g (8oz) button mushrooms, sliced
300ml (½ pint) low-fat natural yogurt
2 tbsps chopped fresh parsley
freshly ground black pepper
pinch of paprika

1 Dry-fry the onion in a preheated non-stick wok or frying pan until soft. Add the garlic and beef, season well and cook until sealed.

2 Sprinkle the flour over, stir well and cook for 1 minute.
3 Add the wine and stock and mix well. Stir in the mustard and mushrooms and simmer for 2–3 minutes to thicken.
4 Remove from the heat, stir in the yogurt and parsley. Dust with paprika before serving.

Beef olives

SERVES 4
1 SERVING 268 KCAL/9G FAT
PREPARATION TIME 15 MINUTES
COOKING TIME 85 MINUTES

Choose thin beef steaks or frying steaks for this tender beef dish in a rich tomato wine sauce.

115g (4oz) lean minced pork
2 garlic cloves, crushed
2 tbsps chopped fresh mixed herbs (rosemary, thyme, oregano)
4 thin-cut beef steaks
2 medium red onions, finely chopped
300ml (½ pint) beef stock
1 wine glass red wine
300ml (½ pint) tomato passata
2 pieces lemon peel
freshly ground black pepper
2 tbsps chopped fresh parsley to garnish

1 Preheat the oven to 170C, 325F, Gas Mark 3.
2 In a small bowl mix together the minced pork with half the crushed garlic and half the mixed herbs, and season with black pepper.

3 Place the 4 steaks on a chopping board. Divide the pork mixture between them and roll up the beef, encasing the pork mixture.

4 In a preheated non-stick pan, dry-fry the beef until browned all over and transfer to an ovenproof dish.

5 Add the onions and the remaining garlic to the pan and cook until soft. Add the beef stock, wine, passata and lemon peel. Pour the mixture over the beef, cover and place in the oven for 1 hour or until the meat is tender.

6 Garnish with the parsley and serve immediately.

Spaghetti bolognese

SERVES 4
1 SERVING 495 KCAL/12.7G FAT
PREPARATION TIME 10 MINUTES
COOKING TIME 45 MINUTES

This classic Italian dish consists of lean minced beef in a rich herby sauce. Traditionally, the beef and onions are fried in olive oil. In this low-fat version the minced beef is dry-fried to release the fat – but not the flavour! For a more robust sauce you can use sun-dried tomatoes instead of canned chopped ones, but make sure you buy the non-oil variety to keep the fat content low.

450g (1lb) lean minced beef
2 garlic cloves, crushed
1 large onion, finely chopped
2 medium carrots, finely grated
2 beef stock cubes

2 × 400g cans chopped tomatoes
4 tbsps tomato purée
1 tbsp chopped fresh oregano or 1 tsp dried oregano
1 vegetable stock cube
350g (12oz) [uncooked weight] spaghetti
freshly ground black pepper
chopped fresh herbs to garnish

1 Preheat a non-stick frying pan or wok. Add the minced beef and dry-fry until it starts to change colour. Remove the mince from the pan and drain through a colander. Wipe out the pan with kitchen paper(it's best to wear an oven glove when you do this, as the pan will be hot).

2 Return the meat to the pan, add the garlic and onion and continue cooking for a further 2–3 minutes, stirring well. Add the carrots and crumble the stock cubes over the top. Add the tomatoes, tomato purée and oregano and mix well to allow the beef stock cubes to dissolve. Reduce the heat to a gentle simmer, season well with black pepper, cover with a lid and continue to simmer gently for 30 minutes until the sauce thickens.

3 Meanwhile, bring a large pan of water to the boil and add a vegetable stock cube. Add the spaghetti and cook until the spaghetti is soft but slightly firm in the centre. Drain through a colander.

4 Arrange the spaghetti on warmed plates, pour the sauce on top and garnish with fresh herbs.

Beef chilli with beer

SERVES 4
1 SERVING 354 KCAL/13.5G FAT
PREPARATION TIME 15 MINUTES
COOKING TIME 40 MINUTES

Adding a small amount of beer to this quick chilli makes a rich, tasty sauce.

2 red onions, finely chopped
2 garlic cloves, crushed
450g (1lb) extra lean minced beef
2–3 fresh chillies, seeded and chopped
1 × 400g can kidney beans, drained and rinsed
1 × 400g can chopped tomatoes
300ml (½ pint) tomato passata
2 tsps chopped fresh oregano
3 tsps vegetable bouillon stock powder
150ml (¼ pint) stout

1 Preheat a non-stick frying pan. Dry-fry the onion and garlic for 1–2 minutes until soft.
2 Add the beef and continue cooking for 5 minutes until well sealed. If there is some liquid in the pan, pour the mixture into a sieve to drain away the fat.
3 Return the meat to the pan and stir in the chillies, kidney beans and then remaining ingredients. Bring to the boil. Reduce the heat and cover. Simmer gently for 30–35 minutes until the sauce thickens and the beef is tender.

Chilli beef linguine

SERVES 4
1 SERVING 279 KCAL/4G FAT
PREPARATION TIME 10 MINUTES
COOKING TIME 20 MINUTES

Spice up your pasta dishes with this easy to prepare bolognese-style sauce.

225g (8oz) [uncooked weight] linguine
1 vegetable stock cube
1 red onion, finely chopped
1 garlic clove, crushed
115g (4oz) lean minced beef
1 small red chilli, finely sliced
600ml (1 pint) tomato passata
1 tbsp chopped fresh mixed herbs
freshly ground black pepper
chopped fresh chives to garnish

1 Cook the linguine in a large pan of boiling water with the vegetable stock cube for extra flavour.
2 In a non-stick pan dry-fry the onion and garlic until soft. Add the beef and cook until it completely changes colour.
3 Add the sliced chilli, the tomato passata and the herbs, season with black pepper and continue cooking for 15–20 minutes until the sauce thickens.
4 Drain the linguine and pour into a warmed serving dish. Spoon the sauce on top and garnish with chopped chives.

Fillet steak with salsa verde

SERVES 4
1 SERVING 263 KCAL/8.9G FAT
PREPARATION TIME 10 MINUTES
COOKING TIME 15–20 MINUTES

4 extra lean fillet steaks (approx. 150g/5oz each)
300ml (½ pint) red wine
1 shallot, finely chopped
1–2 tsps arrowroot
salt and freshly ground black pepper

for the salsa
2 medium red onions, finely chopped
1 garlic clove, crushed
1 green pepper, seeded and finely diced
1 tsp chopped fresh chopped mint
1 tsp chopped fresh parsley
salt and freshly ground black pepper

1 Preheat the oven to 200C, 400F, Gas Mark 6.
2 Make the salsa by mixing all the ingredients together in a
   small bowl, season to taste and allow to stand while cooking
   the beef.
3 Season both sides of the fillet steaks with salt and black
   pepper and place in a preheated frying pan. Seal on both
   sides until lightly browned, then transfer to an ovenproof
   dish. Place in the oven for 8–10 minutes, according to your
   cooking preference.

4 Add the red wine and shallot to the pan and simmer gently for 2–3 minutes until the shallot is soft. Slake the arrowroot with a little cold water and whisk into the sauce.
5 Remove the steaks from the oven and place on a serving plate. Spoon the salsa on top.

Beef with green vegetables stir-fry

SERVES 4
1 SERVING 178 KCAL/4.8G FAT
PREPARATION TIME 10 MINUTES
COOKING TIME 15 MINUTES

2 celery sticks
115g (4oz) fine green beans
115g (4oz) courgettes
115g (4oz) broccoli florets
115g (4oz) asparagus
450g (1lb) lean beef rump, cut into thin strips
2 garlic cloves, crushed
4 tbsps hoisin sauce
2 tbsps lemon juice
2 tbsps dry sherry
1 tbsp chopped fresh parsley

1 Slice the vegetables into fine strips.
2 In a preheated non-stick frying pan dry-fry the beef and garlic for 3–4 minutes. Add the vegetables and cook for a further 4-5 minutes.
3 Stir in the hoisin sauce, lemon juice and sherry. Bring to the boil and sprinkle with parsley. Serve immediately.

Roast beef with Yorkshire pudding and dry-roast sweet potatoes

SERVES 6
1 SERVING BEEF: 218 KCAL/8.3G FAT;
DRY-ROAST SWEET POTATOES: 67 KCAL/0.7G FAT;
YORKSHIRE PUDDING: 79 KCAL/1.3G FAT
PREPARATION TIME 30 MINUTES
COOKING TIME 1–1½ HOURS

1 × 1kg (2lb) joint lean beef (topside)
1 onion, finely diced
1 carrot, diced
1 celery stick, diced
2 tsps mixed dried herbs
600ml (1 pint) beef stock
1 tbsp cornflour
1–2 drops gravy browning

for the dry-roast sweet potatoes
450g (1lb) sweet potatoes, cut in half
1 tbsp soy sauce diluted in 2 tbsps water (optional)

for the Yorkshire pudding batter
115g (4oz) plain flour
1 egg
pinch of salt
150ml (¼ pint) skimmed milk

1 Preheat the oven to 180C, 350F, Gas Mark 4.
2 Prepare the beef by removing as much visible fat as possible.

3 Place the onion, carrot, celery and herbs in the bottom of a roasting tin or ovenproof dish, sit the beef on top and pour 300ml (½ pint) water around. Place in the oven. Allow 15 minutes per 450g (1lb) plus 15 minutes over for rare beef, 20 minutes per 450g (1lb) plus 20 minutes over for medium rare, and 25 minutes per 450g (1lb) plus 30 minutes over if you like your beef well done.

4 Cook the potatoes in boiling water. Drain and place in a non-stick roasting tin. Place in the top of the oven for 35–40 minutes until golden brown. You can baste them with the diluted soy sauce if they appear to dry out.

5 Forty minutes before the beef is ready, make the batter by blending the flour with the egg and a little milk to a smooth paste. Add the salt and whisk in the remaining milk until smooth. Preheat a 6-hole, non-stick Yorkshire pudding tin for 2 minutes in the oven. Remove and half-fill each mould with batter. Increase the oven temperature to 200C, 400F, Gas Mark 6, place the pudding batter in the oven and cook for 35–40 minutes.

6 When the beef is cooked, remove it from the roasting tin and wrap in foil to keep warm. Allow it to rest for 5–10 minutes. Meanwhile, add the beef stock to the pan juices, slake the cornflour with a little water and add to the pan. Stir well as the gravy thickens and add 1–2 drops of gravy browning as required.

7 To serve, carve the beef thinly. Serve with the Yorkshire puddings, dry-roast sweet potatoes, gravy and seasonal vegetables.

Pork

Teriyaki pork with spinach

SERVES 4
1 SERVING 264 KCAL/5.9G FAT
PREPARATION TIME 40 MINUTES
COOKING TIME 2 HOURS

450g (1lb) pork fillet, sliced
2 onions, sliced
2 garlic cloves, crushed
2 tsps chopped fresh ginger
1 tbsp chopped fresh thyme
1 tbsp teriyaki sauce
300ml (½ pint) vegetable stock
2 tbsps tomato purée
450g (1lb) spinach leaves, shredded
sea salt and freshly ground black pepper

1 Season the pork with salt and pepper.
2 In a preheated non-stick wok or frying pan dry-fry the pork
   for 8–10 minutes, turning continuously to brown all sides.
   Remove from the pan and set aside.
3 Add the onions and garlic to the pan and cook until soft.
   Return the pork to the pan and add the ginger, thyme and
   teriyaki sauce. Add the vegetable stock and tomato purée
   and bring the sauce to a gentle simmer.
4 Just before serving, fold in the spinach and remove from the
   heat to allow the spinach to wilt.

Pork and mango meatballs with chilli sauce

SERVES 4
1 SERVING 255 KCAL/11.5G FAT
PREPARATION TIME 10 MINUTES
COOKING TIME 35–40 MINUTES

450g (1lb) lean minced pork
1 medium onion, finely chopped
1 tsp ground cumin
1 tsp ground coriander
1 tbsp chopped fresh parsley
1 tsp salt
freshly ground black pepper
2 tbsps spicy mango chutney

for the sauce
1 × 400g can chopped tomatoes
1 small red chilli, seeded and finely chopped
1 vegetable stock cube
2 tbsps tomato purée
1 tbsp chopped fresh coriander

1 Preheat the oven to 200C, 400F, Gas Mark 6.
2 In a large mixing bowl combine the pork with the other
   ingredients, mixing well with a wooden spoon. Season with
   black pepper.
3 Form the mixture into golfball-sized pieces, roll until smooth
   and place in an ovenproof dish.

4   Combine the sauce ingredients in a saucepan and bring to
    the boil. Pour over the meatballs and place in the oven for
    35–40 minutes.

Charcoal pork slices with barbecue sauce

SERVES 4
1 SERVING 267 KCAL/7G FAT
PREPARATION TIME 10 MINUTES
COOKING TIME 20 MINUTES

4 lean pork steaks
1 tbsp sesame seeds
1 tbsp paprika
1 tbsp ground coriander
salt and freshly ground black pepper

for the barbecue sauce
300ml (½ pint) tomato passata
6 spring onions, finely chopped
2 smoked garlic cloves, crushed
2 tbsps reduced salt soy sauce
zest and juice of 1 lemon
1 tsp smoked paprika
2 tsps caster sugar
½ tsp caraway seeds (optional)

1   Remove any fat from the pork steaks and season on both
    sides with a little salt and black pepper.
2   Mix together the sesame seeds and spices on a large plate.
    Press the pork slices into the spices to coat both sides.

3 Place on the barbecue and cook, turning regularly, for 15–20 minutes, depending on the thickness of the slices. Test if cooked by cutting a pork slice in half.
4 Combine all the sauce ingredients and pour into a serving bowl.
5 Serve the pork slices hot and drizzle the barbecue sauce on top.

Creamy tomato and sage pork steaks

SERVES 4
1 SERVING 226 KCAL/4.7G FAT
PREPARATION TIME 20 MINUTES
COOKING TIME 40 MINUTES

1 medium onion, finely sliced
4 lean pork steaks
2 garlic cloves, crushed
150ml (¼ pint) vegetable stock
1 tbsp plain flour
3 tbsps dry sherry
1 × 400g can chopped tomatoes
1 tbsp chopped fresh sage leaves
115g (4oz) button chestnut mushrooms
2 bay leaves
2 tbsps virtually fat free fromage frais
1 tbsp chopped fresh parsley
salt and freshly ground black pepper

1 Preheat the oven to 190C, 375F, Gas Mark 6.
2 Dry-fry the onion in a non-stick frying pan until soft.

3 Season the pork on both sides and add to the pan to lightly brown on each side. Remove the pork and place in an ovenproof dish.

4 Add the garlic and 2 tbsps of stock to the onions and stir in the flour. 'Cook out' the flour for 1 minute.

5 Add the remaining stock, and the sherry and tomatoes. Stir in the sage leaves, mushrooms and bay leaves and bring to the boil. Pour over the pork and cover with aluminium foil.

6 Place in the centre of the oven for 30–35 minutes.

7 Just before serving, remove the bay leaves, stir in the fromage frais and sprinkle with chopped fresh parsley.

Pork fillet stuffed with apricots

SERVES 4
1 SERVING 408 KCAL/8.4G FAT
PREPARATION TIME 10 MINUTES
COOKING TIME 45 MINUTES

Pork fillet is very lean and cooks quickly either stir-fried or roasted. The apricots add a sweet stuffing, which is complemented with a tomato and sherry sauce.

1kg (2lb) lean pork fillet, fat removed
350g (12oz) ready-to-eat dried apricots, finely chopped
2 garlic cloves, finely chopped
1 tbsp chopped fresh mint
300ml (½ pint) tomato passata
150ml (¼ pint) dry sherry
freshly ground black pepper

1 Preheat the oven to 220C, 425F, Gas Mark 7.
2 Cut down the centre of the pork fillet but not totally right through. Keep making cuts along the length of the meat, opening it out and pressing it flat with your hands until it is completely flat.
3 In a small bowl, mix together the apricots, garlic and mint.
4 Season the meat generously with black pepper and then spread the apricot mixture on top of the meat.
5 Roll up the meat like a Swiss roll and tie with kitchen string. Place in an ovenproof dish and pour the passata and the sherry over.
6 Roast in the oven for 35–40 minutes until cooked. Let the meat relax for 5 minutes, then cut into slices, drizzle with the sauce and serve immediately.

Crunchy bacon and spaghetti

SERVES 1
1 SERVING 357 KCAL/2.5G FAT
PREPARATION TIME 10 MINUTES
COOKING TIME 35 MINUTES

3 thin slices lean smoked bacon
50g (2oz) [uncooked weight] spaghetti
1 small can chopped tomatoes
2 medium mushrooms, thinly sliced
2 tbsps frozen sweetcorn
1 tbsp sweet pickle
2 tsps cornflour
salt and freshly ground black pepper to taste

1 Trim any visible fat from the bacon. Grill the bacon on both sides.
2 Cook the spaghetti in boiling water for 10 minutes. While the spaghetti is cooking, place the tomatoes in a saucepan and add the mushrooms, sweetcorn and pickle. Cook on a moderate heat, then allow to simmer.
3 Wipe off any traces of fat from the bacon with kitchen paper, snip into bite-size pieces and add to the tomato mixture.
4 Dissolve the cornflour in a little cold water and gradually add to the bacon and tomato mixture so that it thickens as it simmers. Season to taste.
5 By the time the spaghetti is cooked, the bacon and tomato mixture will be ready to serve. Drain the spaghetti, place on a serving plate and top with the bacon and tomato mixture.

Gammon with pineapple rice

SERVES 1
1 SERVING 431 KCAL/5.5G FAT
PREPARATION TIME 10 MINUTES
COOKING TIME 20 MINUTES

1 gammon steak
1 small onion, finely chopped
1 small can pineapple chunks in natural juice
½ vegetable stock cube
50g (2oz) [uncooked weight] basmati rice
50g (2oz) canned or frozen peas
½ red pepper, seeded and sliced
dash of soy sauce
1 tbsp chopped fresh chives
salt and freshly ground black pepper

1 Cut the gammon steak into cubes and gently dry-fry with the onion in a non-stick pan.
2 Add the pineapple and juice, the stock cube, rice and approximately 300ml (½ pint) water and bring to the boil. Cover and cook for 10 minutes or until the rice is tender and most of the liquid is absorbed. Add more boiling water during cooking if necessary.
3 Stir in the peas, red pepper and soy sauce and season to taste. Finally, stir in the chives, heat through and serve immediately.

Chorizo jambalaya ❄

SERVES 4
1 SERVING 390 KCAL/8G FAT
PREPARATION TIME 10 MINUTES
COOKING TIME 20 MINUTES

4 lean pork slices
50g (2oz) sliced chorizo
1 medium red onion, finely chopped
2 garlic cloves, crushed
2 celery sticks, finely diced
1 green pepper, seeded and finely chopped
600ml (1 pint) tomato passata
300ml (½ pint) vegetable stock
50g (2oz) [uncooked weight] basmati rice
1 tbsp chopped fresh mixed herbs
salt and freshly ground black pepper

1 Preheat a non-stick pan. Trim away any traces of fat from each pork slice and cut into bite-size pieces. Season with salt and black pepper.
2 Dry-fry the pork in the pan and seal on both sides.
3 Add the chorizo, onion, garlic, celery and green pepper to the pan and cook quickly over a high heat to soften. Add the tomato passata, vegetable stock and rice. Stir well and add the herbs.
4 Cover and simmer for 25 minutes to allow the rice to cook through. Serve immediately.

Lamb

Lamb and pearl barley casserole

SERVES 4
1 SERVING 402 KCAL/10.5G FAT
PREPARATION TIME 15 MINUTES
COOKING TIME 1 HOUR 45 MINUTES

2 medium onions, diced
2 garlic cloves, crushed
450g (1lb) lean diced lamb
4 carrots, diced
1 large turnip, diced
450g (1lb) baby new potatoes
2 celery sticks, chopped
1.2 litres (2 pints) meat stock
bouquet garni
50g (2oz) green lentils, soaked overnight
25g (1oz) haricot beans, soaked overnight
25g (1oz) pearl barley, soaked overnight
freshly ground black pepper
2 tbsps chopped fresh parsley

1 In a preheated non-stick pan, dry-fry the onions and garlic
   for 2–3 minutes until soft. Add the lamb, and season well
   with black pepper. Continue to cook over a high heat until
   well sealed.
2 Transfer to a large casserole dish and add the remaining
   vegetables, stock and bouquet garni.

3 Rinse the lentils, beans and pearl barley well and add to the casserole.
4 Cover and simmer gently for 1 hour or until the meat is tender, topping up with additional stock if required. Sprinkle with fresh parsley and serve.

Rack of lamb with garlic herb crust

SERVES 4
1 SERVING 378 KCAL/18G FAT
PREPARATION TIME 20 MINUTES
COOKING TIME 30 MINUTES

Rack of lamb is delicious but does have quite a thick layer of fat on top. This sweet herby crust keeps the meat moist and adds lots of flavour.

8-rib rack of lamb
1 tbsp redcurrant jelly
2 smoked garlic cloves, crushed
25g (1oz) fresh white breadcrumbs
2 tsps chopped fresh rosemary
2 tsps chopped fresh thyme
2 tsps chopped fresh mint
salt and freshly ground black pepper

1 Preheat the oven to 190C, 375F, Gas Mark 5.
2 Using a sharp knife, remove the fat from the outside of the lamb. In a small bowl mix together the redcurrant jelly and garlic until smooth. Spread the mixture over the lamb.
3 Mix together the breadcrumbs and herbs in a shallow dish.

Season with salt and black pepper. Carefully dip the lamb into the breadcrumbs, pressing down well to make the crumbs stick to the lamb.

4 Place the lamb in a roasting tray and press any remaining crumbs onto the surface of the lamb. Roast in the centre of the oven for 25 minutes.

5 Remove from the oven and allow to stand for 5 minutes.

6 Slice the lamb in between the bones and allow 2 cutlets per person. Serve hot with additional redcurrant jelly.

Lamb burgers

SERVES 4
1 SERVING 237 KCAL/6.8G FAT
PREPARATION TIME 5 MINUTES
COOKING TIME 10 MINUTES

450g (1lb) lean minced lamb
1 small onion, finely chopped
2 tbsps tomato ketchup
salt and freshly ground black pepper

1 Mix all the ingredients together and season well with salt and pepper.

2 Divide the mixture into 4 portions and form into burger shapes.

3 Cook each burger under a very hot grill for 5–6 minutes on each side.

Lamb kofta with creamy chilli dip

SERVES 4
1 SERVING 244 KCAL/16G FAT
PREPARATION TIME 20 MINUTES
COOKING TIME 10 MINUTES

450g (1lb) lean minced lamb
1 smoked garlic clove, crushed
1 tbsp finely chopped fresh mint
1 tbsp finely chopped fresh flat leaf parsley
1 tsp ground cumin
1 tsp ground turmeric
1 tsp ground allspice
1 egg beaten
salt and freshly ground black pepper

for the chilli dip
1 small pot low-fat yogurt
1 smoked garlic clove, crushed
1–2 tsps chilli paste
1 tbsp finely chopped fresh mint

1 In a large bowl mix together the lamb mince, garlic, herbs
   and spices and the beaten egg. Add salt and freshly ground
   black pepper.
2 Using your hands, shape the mixture into 8 balls. Mould the
   balls around skewers to form sausage shapes.
3 Place under a hot grill until browned all over and cooked
   through.
4 Combine all the chilli dip ingredients and place in a small
   serving bowl.
5 Serve the lamb koftas with the dipping sauce.

Pan-fried liver with onions and balsamic vinegar

SERVES 2
1 SERVING 354 KCAL/12.8G FAT
PREPARATION TIME 10 MINUTES
COOKING TIME 25 MINUTES

spray oil
1 tbsp plain flour
450g (1lb) lamb's liver
1 medium onion, finely diced
1 tsp ground coriander
3 tbsps balsamic vinegar
150ml (¼ pint) lamb stock
salt and freshly ground black pepper

1 Preheat the oven to 150C, 3900F, Gas Mark 2. Spray a non-stick frying pan with a little spray oil and heat the pan.
2 Season the flour with salt and pepper and toss the liver in it so that it is well coated. Place the liver in the hot pan to seal on both sides (this will take about 1–2 minutes each side, depending on how thick the slices are).
3 Remove the liver from the pan and place in the oven to continue cooking. Add the onion and coriander to the frying pan and dry-fry until the onion softens. Add the balsamic vinegar.
4 To de-glaze the pan, stir in the stock, scraping any residue from the pan. Just before serving, return the liver to the pan to coat with the sauce.

Poultry

Chicken stuffed with mozzarella and basil

SERVES 4
1 SERVING 356 KCAL/9G FAT
PREPARATION TIME 20 MINUTES
COOKING TIME 40 MINUTES

4 thin slices lean Parma ham
4 skinless chicken breasts
175g (6oz) half-fat mozzarella, sliced
8 large basil leaves
salt and freshly ground black pepper

for the sauce
1 × 400g can chopped tomatoes
4 spring onions
zest and juice of 1 lemon
2 tbsps chopped fresh parsley
1 smoked garlic clove, crushed

1 Preheat the oven to 200C, 400F, Gas Mark 6.
2 Remove any fat from the Parma ham. Place the chicken
   breasts on a chopping board. Using a sharp knife, cut each
   breast across the centre to create a pocket. Season with salt
   and pepper.
3 Place 2 slices of mozzarella and two basil leaves in the centre
   of each breast. Wrap each breast with a slice of Parma ham
   and place in an ovenproof dish.

4 Bake in the oven for 30–35 minutes.
5 Place all the sauce ingredients in a small saucepan and heat gently.
6 Serve the chicken with the sauce.

Spicy chicken drumsticks

SERVES 4
1 SERVING 180 KCAL/9.5G FAT
PREPARATION TIME 10 MINUTES
COOKING TIME 35 MINUTES

Removing the skin from the drumsticks reduces the fat considerably and allows the spices to penetrate the flesh.

8 fresh chicken drumsticks
2 garlic cloves, finely chopped
2 tsps smoked paprika
2 tsps ground coriander
1 tsp ground turmeric
1 tsp ground ginger
salt and freshly ground black pepper

1 Preheat the oven to 200C, 400F, Gas Mark 6.
2 Pull away the skin from the chicken drumsticks and discard.
3 Mix together the spices and place on a plate with the garlic. Press the chicken into the spices, coating all sides of the chicken.
4 Transfer the chicken to a non-stick baking tray and place in a hot oven for 30 minutes until fully cooked. Allow to cool, then pack into an airtight container and refrigerate.

Turmeric chicken

SERVES 4
1 SERVING 280 KCAL/4.9G FAT
PREPARATION TIME 20 MINUTES
COOKING TIME 35 MINUTES

1 medium onion, finely sliced
2 garlic cloves, crushed
4 large skinless chicken breasts, diced
juice of 2 lemons
1 tbsp plain flour
2 tsps ground turmeric
150ml (¼ pint) chicken stock
3 tbsps dry white wine
225g (8oz) green beans, cut in half
salt and freshly ground black pepper
1 tbsp chopped fresh parsley to garnish

1 Dry-fry the onion and garlic in a preheated non-stick frying pan until soft.
2 Season the chicken with a little salt and plenty of black pepper, add to the pan and lightly brown on each side.
3 Add the lemon juice, and stir in the flour and the turmeric. 'Cook out' the flour for 1 minute.
4 Slowly stir in the stock, wine and green beans. Bring to the boil then reduce the heat to a gentle simmer. Cover with a lid and simmer for 15 minutes until the beans are cooked.
5 Spoon into a serving dish and garnish with the parsley.

Spicy chicken pasta

SERVES 4
1 SERVING 336 KCAL/3.4G FAT
PREPARATION TIME 20 MINUTES
COOKING TIME 30 MINUTES

225g (8oz) [uncooked weight] rigatoni pasta
1 vegetable stock cube
1 red onion, finely chopped
2 garlic cloves, crushed
225g (8oz) minced chicken
1 red pepper, seeded and finely diced
1 × 400g can chopped tomatoes
1 red chilli, seeded and finely chopped
8–10 basil leaves
225g (8oz) fresh young spinach leaves
salt and freshly ground black pepper
shredded basil leaves to garnish

1 Cook the pasta in boiling water with the vegetable stock
   cube.
2 Meanwhile in a non-stick frying pan dry-fry the onion for
   2–3 minutes until soft, add the garlic and minced chicken
   and cook for a further 8 minutes.
3 Add the red pepper, the tomatoes and the chilli, and bring
   the sauce to a gentle simmer. Season to taste with salt and
   black pepper. Just before serving stir in the spinach leaves
   until wilted.
4 Drain the pasta and pour into a serving dish. Spoon the
   sauce over and sprinkle with shredded basil leaves.

Chicken jalfrezi ❄

SERVES 4
1 SERVING 288 KCAL/5G FAT
PREPARATION TIME 10 MINUTES
COOKING TIME 25 MINUTES

You can substitute diced beef or lamb for the chicken. Just allow 20 minutes extra cooking time to allow the meat to tenderise. For vegetarians, Quorn fillets work really well.

4 skinless chicken breasts
1 tsp ground cumin
1 tsp ground coriander
2 tsps garam masala
1 × 2.5cm (1in) piece fresh ginger, finely chopped
2 red onions, diced
1 red and 1 green pepper, seeded and diced
2 garlic cloves, crushed
1 small red chilli, sliced
juice of 1 lime
2 tsps vegetable bouillon stock powder
600ml (1 pint) tomato passata
1 tbsp chopped fresh coriander
salt and freshly ground black pepper
1 tbsp chopped fresh mint to garnish

1 Slice the chicken into bite-size pieces, season with a little salt and black pepper and place in a bowl. Add the cumin, ground coriander, garam masala and ginger and mix well.
2 Preheat a non-stick wok until hot. Dry-fry the onions, peppers and garlic for 2–3 minutes until they start to colour.

3 Add the chicken and continue cooking for 5–6 minutes as the chicken starts to change colour. Add the remaining ingredients except the fresh coriander and mint. Reduce the heat and simmer gently for 20 minutes.
4 Just before serving stir in the coriander and mint. Spoon into a warmed serving dish and garnish with mint leaves.

Pan-fried chicken in white wine

SERVES 4
1 SERVING 230 KCAL/4.9G FAT
PREPARATION TIME 5 MINUTES
COOKING TIME 20 MINUTES

4 chicken breasts (approx. 130g/4½oz each), sliced
115g (4oz) mushrooms, sliced
1 × 295g can Campbell's chicken and white wine soup
250ml (8fl oz) semi-skimmed milk
1 tbsp chopped fresh parsley

1 Dry-fry the chicken in a preheated non-stick pan for 5 minutes.
2 Add the mushrooms to the pan and cook for a further 5 minutes.
3 Stir in the remaining ingredients and simmer for a further 10 minutes, stirring gently.

Chicken with fresh wild mushrooms

SERVES 4
1 SERVING 272 KCAL/4.3G FAT
PREPARATION TIME 20 MINUTES
COOKING TIME 40 MINUTES

*Many supermarkets now stock fresh wild and exotic
mushrooms. This recipe works equally well with pork steaks or
Quorn fillets.*

4 lean skinless chicken breasts (approx. 120g each)
1 medium red onion, finely chopped
1 × 2.5cm (1in) piece of fresh ginger, peeled and
   finely chopped
1 chicken stock cube, dissolved in 300ml (½ pint) water
1 tbsp plain flour
225g (8oz) fresh wild mushrooms, sliced
1 wine glass dry white wine
1 tbsp chopped fresh thyme
1 tbsp virtually fat free fromage frais
salt and freshly ground black pepper

1 Preheat a non-stick frying pan. Season the chicken breasts
   on both sides with salt and black pepper and place in the
   pan. Dry-fry the chicken on both sides for 5–6 minutes until
   lightly browned, then remove from the pan and transfer to a
   plate.
2 Add the onion to the pan and cook gently until lightly
   coloured. Add the ginger and 2 tbsps of the stock. Sprinkle
   the flour over and 'cook out' for 1 minute. Gradually stir in
   the remaining stock, along with the mushrooms and the wine.

3 Return the chicken to the pan and add the thyme. Simmer
   gently for 15–20 minutes until the sauce has reduced and
   the chicken cooked through.
4 Just before serving, remove the pan from the heat and stir in
   the fromage frais.

Chicken tagine with orange

SERVES 4
1 SERVING 280 KCAL/4.6G FAT
PREPARATION TIME 20 MINUTES
COOKING TIME 45 MINUTES

*This aromatic, slow-cooked chicken dish brings a Moroccan
touch to the table.*

1 medium onion, finely chopped
4 large skinless chicken breasts
2 garlic cloves, crushed
150ml (¼ pint) chicken stock
1 tbsp plain flour
zest and juice of 1 orange
1 × 400g can chopped tomatoes
1 tbsp chopped fresh thyme
1 small red chilli, sliced
freshly ground black pepper
chopped fresh parsley to garnish

1 Preheat the oven to 180C, 350F, Gas Mark 4.
2 Dry-fry the onion in a non-stick pan until soft. Season the
   chicken breasts on both sides with black pepper and add to

the pan. Lightly brown them on each side. Remove the chicken and place in an ovenproof dish.

3 Add the garlic and 2 tbsps of stock to the onion, stir in the flour and 'cook out' for 1 minute. Add the remaining stock, the orange zest and juice and the tomatoes. Stir in the thyme and chilli and bring to the boil. Pour over the chicken and cover with foil.

4 Place in the centre of the oven for 30–35 minutes. Sprinkle with fresh parsley.

Spicy chicken stir-fry

SERVES 4
1 SERVING 220 KCAL/3.5G FAT
PREPARATION TIME 10 MINUTES
COOKING TIME 15 MINUTES

450g (1lb) skinless chicken fillets, cut into strips
1 medium red onion, finely sliced
1 red pepper, seeded and sliced
2 small courgettes, sliced
115g (4oz) chestnut mushrooms, sliced
1 tsp chopped fresh ginger
1 tbsp reduced-salt soy sauce
1 tbsp hot mango chutney
2 tsps finely chopped lemongrass
freshly ground black pepper to taste

1 Preheat a non-stick wok or frying pan. Add the chicken strips and season well with freshly ground black pepper. Stir-fry for 5–6 minutes or until just cooked.

2 Add the onion, red pepper and courgettes and stir-fry for 2–3 minutes, tossing the vegetables in the wok. Add the mushrooms and ginger and mix well.
3 Mix together the soy sauce, mango chutney and the lemongrass and add to the pan, coating the chicken and vegetables. Serve immediately.

Turkey and pepper stroganoff

SERVES 4
1 SERVING 280 KCAL/3.4G FAT
PREPARATION TIME 30 MINUTES
COOKING TIME 15 MINUTES

450g (1lb) lean cooked turkey flesh, cut into strips
1 medium onion, chopped
1 red pepper, seeded and diced
2 garlic cloves, crushed
300ml (½ pint) chicken stock
1 tbsp plain flour
150ml (¼ pint) Madeira wine
225g (8oz) small chestnut mushrooms, sliced
2 tsps Dijon mustard
300ml (½ pint) virtually fat free fromage frais
2 tbsps chopped fresh parsley
freshly ground black pepper
pinch of paprika to dust

1 Dry-fry the cooked turkey and onion in a non-stick pan or wok for 2–3 minutes.
2 Add the red pepper and garlic and cook for 1 minute.

3 Add half the stock and sprinkle the flour over. Mix well and
   cook for 1 minute.
4 Add the remaining stock and the Madeira wine. Stir in the
   mushrooms and mustard and cook for 2–3 minutes.
5 Remove from the heat, stir in the fromage frais and parsley.
   Season to taste and dust with paprika before serving.

Turkey lasagne

SERVES 4
1 SERVING 447 KCAL/9G FAT
PREPARATION TIME 30 MINUTES
COOKING TIME 80 MINUTES

225g (8oz) minced turkey
1 large red onion, finely diced
2 garlic cloves, crushed
1 red pepper, seeded and cut into dice
6 fresh ripe tomatoes, cut into quarters
2 tbsps chopped fresh oregano
1 × 400g can chopped tomatoes
300ml (½ pint) passata
225g (8oz) no pre-cook lasagne sheets
salt and freshly ground black pepper

for the topping
300ml (½ pint) low-fat natural yogurt
1 egg, beaten
1 tsp English mustard powder
2 tsps finely grated Parmesan cheese
salt and freshly ground black pepper

1 Preheat the oven to 200C, 400F, Gas Mark 6.
2 Dry-fry the turkey, onion and garlic in a preheated non-stick wok or pan for 8–10 minutes until lightly browned. Season with salt and black pepper. Add the red pepper, the fresh tomatoes and the oregano. Stir in the canned tomatoes and the passata and simmer for 15 minutes.
3 Spoon a thin layer of the tomato sauce into an ovenproof dish. Cover with a layer of lasagne sheets. Do not overlap them, as they will expand during cooking. Continue layering with the remaining sauce and pasta sheets.
4 Combine all the topping ingredients, spread over the top of the lasagne and sprinkle with the Parmesan cheese. Bake in the oven for 35–40 minutes until brown.

Fish and seafood

Broccoli and smoked salmon spaghetti

SERVES 4
1 SERVING 275 KCAL/3G FAT
PREPARATION TIME 20 MINUTES
COOKING TIME 30 MINUTES

*This is a great way to use up left over cooked broccoli and other
vegetables.*

225g (8oz) small broccoli florets
225g (8oz) [uncooked weight] spaghetti
1 vegetable stock cube
8 spring onions, finely chopped
1 garlic clove, crushed
1 red pepper, seeded and finely diced
115g (4oz) smoked salmon, sliced into strips
juice of 1 lemon
2 tbsps chopped fresh flat leaf parsley
salt and freshly ground black pepper

1   Place a large pan of salted water on to boil. Blanch the
    broccoli for 2 minutes. Using a slotted spoon, remove from
    the pan.
2   Cook the pasta in boiling water with the vegetable stock
    cube.
3   Meanwhile in a non-stick frying pan dry-fry the onions for
    2–3 minutes until soft. Add the garlic and red pepper and
    cook for a further 5 minutes.

4 Add the broccoli, salmon and lemon juice, and toss well. Season to taste.
5 Drain the spaghetti, add to the pan and toss well. Pour into a serving dish and sprinkle with flat leaf parsley.

Quick tuna pâté

SERVES 1
1 SERVING 276 KCAL/2.8G FAT
PREPARATION TIME 10 MINUTES

225g canned tuna in brine
75g (3oz) low-fat yogurt
2 tbsps reduced-oil salad dressing
2 tsps lemon juice
1 tsp chopped fresh or freeze-dried dill
¼ tsp cayenne pepper
1 lemon slice
salt and freshly ground black pepper

1 Drain the tuna well and place in a bowl. Add the yogurt, reduced-oil dressing and lemon juice. Mash with a fork until well combined. Add the fresh dill and cayenne pepper and season with salt and pepper. Mix well.
2 Spoon the mixture into a dish and place a slice of lemon on top. Refrigerate for at least 2 hours before serving.

Potted smoked trout

SERVES 4
1 SERVING 96 KCAL/3.2G FAT
PREPARATION TIME 15 MINUTES

225g (8oz) fresh smoked trout fillets
1 tbsp Dijon mustard
115g (4oz) Quark (low-fat soft cheese)
1 tbsp chopped fresh parsley
freshly ground black pepper
bunch of watercress to serve

1 Break up the trout fillets with a fork in a small bowl. Add the
  mustard, Quark and parsley. Mix well and season with freshly
  ground black pepper.
2 Press the mixture into 4 small ramekin dishes and smooth
  the tops over with a knife. Refrigerate until ready to serve.

Baked halibut steak with sage and Parma ham

SERVES 4
1 SERVING 170 KCAL/4.3G FAT
PREPARATION TIME 5 MINUTES
COOKING TIME 10 MINUTES

4×115g (4×4oz) halibut steaks
juice of 1 lemon
12 sage leaves
4 thin slices Parma ham
salt and freshly ground black pepper

for the horseradish sauce
2 tbsps grated fresh horseradish
2 tbsps virtually fat free fromage frais
salt and cracked black pepper

1 Preheat the oven to 200C, 400F, Gas Mark 6.
2 Place the halibut steaks in an ovenproof dish. Season each
   steak on both sides with salt and black pepper and drizzle
   with lemon juice. Place 3 sage leaves on top of each steak
   and cover each with a slice of Parma ham.
3 Bake in the oven for 6–8 minutes until just cooked.
4 Combine the horseradish sauce ingredients in a small bowl
   and spoon over the steaks.

Pan-fried tuna with pepper noodles

SERVES 4
1 SERVING 356 KCAL/8.6G FAT
PREPARATION TIME 10 MINUTES
COOKING TIME 20 MINUTES

4 fresh tuna steaks
225g (8oz) [uncooked weight] thread noodles
1 tsp vegetable oil
1 garlic clove, crushed
1 red pepper, seeded and finely sliced
1 yellow pepper, seeded and finely sliced
zest and juice of 1 lime
1 tbsp light soy sauce
freshly ground black pepper
4 lime slices and red pepper to garnish

1 Trim the tuna steaks with a sharp knife, removing any unsightly dark flesh. Season well with black pepper.

2 Prepare the noodles by placing in boiling water for 2–3 minutes. Drain and refresh under cold running water.

3 Heat a griddle pan or non-stick frying pan, add the vegetable oil and then wipe out the pan with a piece of kitchen paper, taking care not to burn your fingers (use an oven glove if necessary).

4 Place the tuna, best side down, in the hot pan. As the tuna cooks it will change colour. Rather like a thermometer, the colour band will change and move up the fish. When it reaches halfway up the steaks, turn the steaks over and cook for a few minutes. Remove from the pan and place in a warm oven to keep hot.

5 Add the garlic and peppers to the pan and sauté quickly until they start to soften. Add the noodles, lime zest and juice and soy sauce. Cook for 1–2 minutes, turning regularly.

6 Place the noodles on warmed serving plates and top with the tuna steaks. Garnish with a slice of lime and red pepper.

Baked smoked haddock with spinach, tomato and ginger

SERVES 4
1 SERVING 191 KCAL/2G FAT
PREPARATION TIME 25 MINUTES
COOKING TIME 35 MINUTES

The simple and versatile tomato sauce used here is very low in fat. It is ideal for coating oven-baked fish or to use as a topping sauce for pasta.

3 baby leeks, finely chopped
150ml (¼ pint) dry white wine
2 × 400g cans chopped tomatoes
1 × 2.5cm (1in) piece ginger, finely chopped
2 tsps vegetable bouillon stock powder
225g (8oz) fresh spinach
4 smoked haddock fillets
freshly ground black pepper

1 Preheat the oven to 180C, 350F, Gas Mark 4. Preheat a non-stick pan until hot.
2 Dry-fry the leeks in the preheated hot pan until soft. Add the wine, tomatoes, ginger and stock powder and simmer gently for 15 minutes until the sauce has reduced.
3 Chop the spinach and place in the bottom of an ovenproof dish. Season the fish on both sides with black pepper and place on top of the spinach.
4 Pour the sauce over the fish and cover with a piece of greaseproof paper.
5 Bake in the oven for 6–8 minutes until firm but not overcooked.

Fisherman's pie

SERVES 6
1 SERVING 258 KCAL/2G FAT
PREPARATION TIME 20 MINUTES
COOKING TIME 1 HOUR

675g (1½lb) potatoes
1 vegetable stock cube
2 tbsps low-fat natural yogurt
350g (12oz) smoked haddock
350g (12oz) cod or white haddock
225g (8oz) cooked shelled prawns
2 baby leeks, chopped
150ml (¼ pint) fish stock
1 tbsp flour
½ wine glass white wine
1 tbsp Dijon mustard
600ml (1 pint) skimmed milk
2 tbsps capers
salt and freshly ground black pepper
chopped fresh parsley to garnish

1 Preheat the oven to 220C, 425F, Gas Mark 7.
2 Cook the potatoes in a saucepan of boiling water with the
   vegetable stock cube. Drain and mash until smooth. Mix in
   the yogurt and season with salt and black pepper.
3 Remove the skin and bones from the fish. Cut into bite-sized
   pieces and place in the bottom of an ovenproof dish. Add
   the prawns.
4 Place the leeks and the fish stock in a medium saucepan and
   cook for 1–2 minutes. Sprinkle the flour over and mix well.

Cook for a further minute in order to 'cook out' the flour. Add the wine and mustard and beat well. Gradually add the skimmed milk, stirring continuously to prevent any lumps from forming. Bring to the boil, allowing the sauce to thicken. Pour over the fish and sprinkle the capers on top. Allow to cool for 20 minutes, then cover with the mashed potato using a fork or a piping bag with a large star nozzle.

5 Place in the oven for 30–40 minutes until golden. Just before serving, sprinkle with the chopped parsley.

Smoked haddock pasta

SERVES 4
1 SERVING 383 KCAL/2.2G FAT
PREPARATION TIME 10 MINUTES
COOKING TIME 40 MINUTES

Naturally smoked haddock is much lighter in colour than yellow haddock which is dipped in dye to colour the outside of the fish.

225g (8oz) [uncooked weight] pasta shapes
4 tail fillets naturally smoked haddock, skinned and boned
300ml (½ pint) skimmed milk
1 red onion, finely chopped
2 garlic cloves, crushed
1 red pepper, seeded and finely chopped
1 red chilli, seeded and finely chopped
3 tsps cornflour
300ml (½ pint) virtually fat-free fromage frais
juice of ½ lemon
8–10 basil leaves
salt and freshly ground black pepper

1 Preheat the oven to 180C, 350F, Gas Mark 5.

2 Cook the pasta in boiling salted water. Drain and set aside.

3 Poach the fish in the milk for 10–15 minutes, and then set aside to cool in the cooking liquor.

4 In a non-stick frying pan, dry-fry the onion for 2–3 minutes until soft. Add the garlic and red pepper and cook for 2–3 minutes. Add the fish, cooking liquor and chilli, and simmer gently.

5 Slake the cornflour with a little cold milk, then gradually whisk into the sauce. Season to taste with salt and pepper.

6 Place the pasta in a bowl and pour the sauce over. Mix in the fromage frais, then flake the fish into the pasta mix. Add the lemon juice and basil and mix well.

7 Spoon into a serving dish and bake in the oven for 15–20 minutes to heat through.

Steamed sea bass with chilli

SERVES 4
1 SERVING 103 KCAL/2.6G FAT
PREPARATION TIME 10 MINUTES
COOKING TIME APPROX. 7 MINUTES

4 sea bass steaks
4 spring onions, sliced
1 × 2.5cm (1in) piece root ginger, finely chopped
1 garlic clove, finely chopped
2 red chillies, finely sliced
1 tsp lime juice
salt and freshly ground black pepper

1 Season the sea bass with salt and pepper and place in the top of a steamer.
2 Scatter the spring onions, ginger, garlic and chilli over the fish. Sprinkle the lime juice over the fish.
3 Steam the fish gently for about 5 minutes or until the fish turns pale pink and is just flaky.

Griddled swordfish with horseradish cream

SERVES 4
1 SERVING 246 KCAL/8G FAT
PREPARATION TIME 10 MINUTES
COOKING TIME 10 MINUTES

Swordfish and tuna steaks are now readily available in most supermarkets. They make the perfect quick meal served with some tasty simple vegetables.

4 fresh swordfish steaks
225g (8oz) fresh fine green beans, cut in half
1 × 115g (4oz) pack cooked beetroot
1 small red onion, finely sliced
2 tbsps low-fat fromage frais
2 tsps horseradish sauce
1 tbsp finely chopped fresh chives
salt and freshly ground black pepper

1 Season the steaks with salt and black pepper and set aside.
2 Cook the green beans in a pan of lightly salted water until tender. Drain, rinse with cold water and place in a bowl.

3 Chop the beetroot into small wedges and add to the beans along with the red onion.

4 Preheat a non-stick griddle pan until hot. Add the steaks and cook for 2–3 minutes on both sides. Remove from the pan, place on a chopping board and allow to rest for 2 minutes.

5 Mix together the fromage frais, horseradish and chives and season with salt and black pepper.

6 Divide the bean salad between 4 bowls, place a swordfish steak on top of each and top with the horseradish cream.

Pan-fried sole with lemon, spinach and tomato pesto

SERVES 4
1 SERVING 224 KCAL/4.6G FAT
PREPARATION TIME 20 MINUTES
COOKING TIME 15 MINUTES

4 fillets Dover sole, cut in half
olive oil spray
225g (8oz) small leaf spinach
juice of 1 lemon

for the pesto
225g (8oz) sundried tomatoes (non-oil variety)
1 tbsp chopped fresh coriander
1 tsp ground coriander
salt and freshly ground black pepper

1 To make the pesto, place the sundried tomatoes in a saucepan and cover with water. Heat until boiling, then reduce the heat and simmer gently for 10 minutes until soft.

2 Allow to cool, then pour into a food processor. Add the fresh and ground coriander and process until smooth, adding more water to provide a sauce-like consistency. Scrape out into a saucepan to keep warm.
3 Preheat a non-stick griddle pan until hot and lightly spray with spray oil. Season the fish on both sides with salt and black pepper, add to the pan and cook over a high heat for 2–3 minutes on each side. Remove from the pan and cover to keep warm.
4 Add the spinach to the pan and wilt, stirring continuously. Add the lemon juice and transfer to a serving dish. Arrange the fish on top and spoon the tomato pesto over.

Blackened tuna with honey and ginger beansprouts

SERVES 4
1 SERVING 229 KCAL/6.2G FAT
PREPARATION TIME 25 MINUTES
COOKING TIME 15 MINUTES

The black onion seeds used in this recipe add a real kick to the tuna. Try them on meat steaks, chicken and to pep up roasted vegetables. Fresh tuna is low in fat and very substantial, so do give it a try.

4 fresh tuna steaks

for the marinade
4 tbsps light soy sauce
zest and juice of 2 limes

3 tsps black onion seeds
1 small red chilli, finely sliced
2 tsps finely chopped lemongrass
salt and freshly ground black pepper

for the beansprouts
1 × 400g pack beansprouts
6 spring onions, finely sliced
4 ripe tomatoes
1 × 2.5cm (1in) piece fresh ginger, peeled and finely chopped
2 tsps rice wine vinegar
2 tsps runny honey
salt and freshly ground black pepper

1 Place the tuna steaks in a shallow dish.
2 Combine the marinade ingredients in a small bowl and pour
   over the tuna steaks. Leave to marinate for 20 minutes.
3 Skin the tomatoes by plunging them into boiling water for 10
   seconds. Remove and submerge in ice cold water. Peel away
   the skin, then slice each tomato in half and remove the seeds
   with a tsp. Chop the tomato flesh and set aside.
4 Preheat a non-stick griddle pan and lightly grease with a
   little olive oil spray, removing the excess with kitchen paper.
5 When the pan is very hot, carefully add the tuna and season
   with salt and black pepper. Cook it quickly for 4–5 minutes
   on each side (if overcooked, the texture will become tough
   and rubbery). Remove from the pan and keep warm.
6 Add the beansprouts to the pan and add the remaining
   ingredients. Toss well until hot enough to serve. Spoon the
   beansprouts onto a serving plate and arrange the tuna steaks
   on top.

Tuna and tarragon pasta

SERVES 1
1 SERVING 389 KCAL/2.6G FAT
PREPARATION TIME 10 MINUTES
COOKING TIME 30 MINUTES

50g (2oz) [uncooked weight] pasta
1 × 185g can tuna in brine
1 tbsp chopped fresh tarragon
1 tbsp tarragon vinegar or cider vinegar
1 tbsp tomato ketchup
1 tomato, chopped
50g (2oz) canned peas, drained
50g (2oz) canned sweetcorn, drained
freshly ground black pepper

1 Cook the pasta in boiling salted water for 8 minutes.
2 Meanwhile, drain and flake the tuna and mix with the
   chopped tarragon, vinegar and tomato ketchup.
3 Place the tomato, peas, sweetcorn and tuna and tarragon
   mixture in a saucepan. Mix well and heat thoroughly.
4 Drain the pasta and top with the tuna sauce. Season to taste
   with freshly ground black pepper.

Prawn risotto

SERVES 4
1 SERVING 372 KCAL/3.5G FAT
PREPARATION TIME 10 MINUTES
COOKING TIME 25 MINUTES

2 garlic cloves, crushed
1 medium onion, finely chopped
225g (8oz) [uncooked weight] basmati rice
pinch of saffron
600ml (1 pint) vegetable stock
½ wine glass white wine
450g (1lb) uncooked large prawn tails, peeled
2 spring onions, finely sliced
2 tbsps Normandy low-fat fromage frais
salt and freshly ground black pepper

1 In a non-stick pan, dry-fry the onion and garlic until soft.
   Add the rice and saffron.
2 Gradually stir in the stock and wine, allowing the rice to
   absorb it before adding more – this will take between 15
   and 20 minutes.
3 Once all the liquid has been added, stir in the prawns. Cover,
   allowing the prawns to cook in the steam for 5–6 minutes.
4 Remove from the heat and fold in the spring onions and
   fromage frais. Season with salt and black pepper to taste.

Smoked ham and prawn jambalya

SERVES 4
1 SERVING 225 KCAL/3.1G FAT
PREPARATION TIME 10 MINUTES
COOKING TIME 20 MINUTES

2 medium onions, chopped
2 garlic cloves, crushed
2 celery sticks, diced
1 × 400g can chopped tomatoes
2 tbsps tomato purée
1 red chilli, seeded and finely chopped
225g (8oz) cooked basmati rice
225g (8oz) smoked ham, cut into bite-sized pieces
225g (8oz) cooked shelled prawns
1 tbsp chopped fresh mixed herbs (e.g. chives, parsley
    and tarragon)
grated fresh nutmeg
salt and freshly ground black pepper

1 Dry-fry the onion and garlic in a non-stick pan until soft.
2 Add the celery, tomatoes, tomato purée and chilli and
   simmer for 10 minutes.
3 Add the rice, smoked ham, prawns, grated nutmeg and herbs
   and simmer for a further 2–3 minutes, making sure the ham
   and prawns are heated through. Season to taste.

Spicy prawn masala

SERVES 4
1 SERVING 146 KCAL/1.5G FAT
PREPARATION TIME 25 MINUTES
COOKING TIME 20 MINUTES

For a vegetarian option, you can use Quorn pieces or a
selection of root vegetables instead of the prawns.

1 large red onion, finely chopped
2 tbsps tomato purée
600ml (1 pint) fish or vegetable stock
1 tbsp tamarind paste
4 kaffir lime leaves
450g (1lb) uncooked shelled prawns
2 tbsps chopped fresh coriander
a little virtually fat free fromage frais

for the paste
3 garlic cloves, peeled
3 tsps ground coriander
½ tsp ground turmeric
½ tsp ground fenugreek
2–3 small whole fresh chillies
seeds removed from 4 crushed cardamom pods
   (discard the pods)

1 Make the paste by grinding all the ingredients in a food
   processor or liquidiser. Scrape the paste into a bowl, then
   rinse out with a little stock.

2 In a non-stick pan dry-fry the onion until soft then add the paste and cook for 2 minutes, stirring continuously.
3 Add the remaining ingredients, except the coriander and the fromage frais, and simmer gently for 15–20 minutes until the sauce thickens and the prawns are cooked through.
4 Just before serving, remove from the heat and stir in the coriander and fromage frais.

Thai prawn rice

SERVES 2
1 SERVING 320 KCAL/1.9G FAT
PREPARATION TIME 5 MINUTES
COOKING TIME 25 MINUTES

115g (4oz) [uncooked weight] basmati rice
1 vegetable stock cube
115g (4oz) cooked shelled king prawns
4 spring onions, sliced
115g (4oz) fine green beans, cut in half
50g (2oz) baby corn, sliced
3 tbsps lime and coriander dressing
sprigs of fresh coriander and slices of fresh lime to garnish

1 Cook the rice in boiling water with the vegetable stock cube.
2 Gently dry-fry the prawns, baby corn, spring onions, and green beans in a preheated non-stick frying pan with a little black pepper. Add the cooked rice and dressing and heat through.
3 Serve with additional dressing if required and garnish with fresh coriander and fresh lime.

Vegetarian

Lemon and mustard seed humous Ⓥ

SERVES 4
1 SERVING 148 KCAL/4.7G FAT
PREPARATION TIME 10 MINUTES
COOKING TIME 15 MINUTES

1 × 425g can chickpeas with no added salt or sugar
300ml (½ pint) soya milk
2 garlic cloves, crushed
2 tsps mustard seed
juice of 1 lemon
salt
cayenne pepper to taste

1 Drain and rinse the chickpeas and place in a food processor.
2 Pour in the milk, garlic and mustard seed and process until
   smooth. Season with salt and pepper, add the lemon juice
   then blend again to combine. Adjust the consistency with a
   little extra milk if required and adjust the seasoning to taste.

Sweetcorn and pepper fajitas ⓥ

SERVES 4
1 SERVING 232 KCAL/1.2G FAT
PREPARATION TIME 20 MINUTES

Tortilla wraps make excellent sandwich substitutes. Make up in advance and wrap well with food wrap. Vary the fillings by adding canned tuna or cooked meat if you wish.

1 × 285g can sweetcorn, drained
225g (8oz) Quark (low-fat soft cheese)
2 tbsps low-fat salad dressing
1 garlic clove, crushed
2 tbsps chopped fresh chives
juice of 1 lime
salt and freshly ground black pepper
4 flat round tortilla breads
1 red and 1 yellow pepper, seeded and finely sliced

1 In a small bowl, combine the sweetcorn, Quark, salad dressing, garlic, chives and lime juice, and season with salt and black pepper. Mix well together.
2 Place the tortilla breads on a chopping board and spread with the mixture. Cover with the sliced peppers. Roll up tightly and slice in half diagonally. Chill until ready to serve.

Grilled pepper and herb pittas Ⓥ

SERVES 4
1 SERVING 311 KCAL/5.6G FAT
PREPARATION TIME 10 MINUTES
COOKING TIME 10 MINUTES

Pitta breads make ideal lightweight pizza bases. They can be stored frozen and defrost really quickly under the grill.

4 pitta breads
150ml (¼ pint) tomato passata
1 tbsp finely chopped mixed fresh herbs (e.g. parsley, chives, basil)
2 tbsps Quark (low-fat soft cheese)
2 tbsps grated low-fat Cheddar cheese
2 spring onions, finely chopped
1 small red pepper, seeded and finely diced
1 tbsp Worcestershire sauce
2 large ripe tomatoes, sliced
salt and freshly ground black pepper

1 Using a sharp knife, score across each pitta bread several times.
2 Spread the passata over the base of each pitta bread and sprinkle with the fresh herbs.
3 In a small bowl combine the cheeses, spring onions and red pepper. Add the Worcestershire sauce and season well with salt and black pepper.
4 Spread the mixture onto the pitta breads and arrange slices of tomato on top.
5 Place under a preheated hot grill until golden brown.
6 Serve immediately with salad.

Italian toast toppers Ⓥ

SERVES 2
1 SERVING 248 KCAL/2.6G FAT
PREPARATION TIME 5 MINUTES
COOKING TIME 15 MINUTES

4 slices multigrain bread
1 medium onion, thinly sliced
1 red pepper, seeded and finely sliced
2 garlic cloves, crushed
1 courgette, finely sliced
115g (4oz) chestnut mushrooms, sliced
1 × 200g can chopped tomatoes
1 tbsp chopped fresh oregano
salt and freshly ground black pepper

1 Toast the bread on both sides very lightly and set aside.
2 Preheat a non-stick frying pan, and dry-fry the onion for 2–3
   minutes until soft. Add the onion, pepper, garlic, courgette
   and mushrooms and cook briskly over a high heat, turning
   them over regularly.
3 Stir in the tomatoes and herbs and simmer gently for 5–6
   minutes until the liquid has reduced to leave a thick, chunky
   paste. Spread the mixture onto the toasted bread and place
   under a hot grill for 2–3 minutes to brown. Serve hot.

Three pepper frittata ⓥ

SERVES 2
1 SERVING 167 KCAL/10G FAT
PREPARATION TIME 5 MINUTES
COOKING TIME 10 MINUTES

½ red and ½ yellow pepper, seeded and diced
3 eggs
2 tbsps skimmed milk
1 tbsp finely chopped parsley
1 tbsp light soy sauce
freshly ground black pepper

1 Preheat a non-stick frying pan, add the peppers and dry-fry
   for 2–3 minutes until lightly coloured, seasoning well with
   black pepper.
2 In a mixing bowl whisk the eggs and gradually add the milk,
   parsley and soy sauce.
3 Pour the mixture into the frying pan, reduce the heat and
   cook gently until the frittata is just set. Fold the frittata in
   half and slide onto a warmed serving plate.

Baked ginger stuffed tomatoes Ⓥ

SERVES 2
1 SERVING 129 KCAL/1.6G FAT
PREPARATION TIME 10 MINUTES
COOKING TIME 30 MINUTES

4 large ripe beef tomatoes
1 medium onion, finely diced
1 red pepper, seeded and diced
2 garlic cloves, crushed
1 tbsp chopped fresh ginger
1 × 200g can chopped tomatoes
1 tbsp chopped chervil
salt and freshly ground black pepper

1 Preheat the oven to 190C, 375F, Gas Mark 5.
2 Slice off the tops of the tomatoes and reserve. Using a
   dessertspoon, remove the inner core and seeds from the
   tomatoes and reserve. Place the tomato shells in an
   ovenproof dish.
3 Preheat a non-stick frying pan and dry-fry the onion for 2–3
   minutes until soft. Add the pepper, garlic and ginger and
   cook for a further 2–3 minutes. Stir in the reserved tomato
   inner core and seeds, the chopped tomatoes and herbs and
   simmer until the sauce thickens, seasoning with salt and
   black pepper.
4 Spoon the cooked mixture into the tomato shells and place a
   tomato top over each one. Bake in the oven for 20 minutes.
   Serve hot or cold.

Indonesian rice Ⓥ

SERVES 6
1 SERVING 161 KCAL/0.6G FAT
PREPARATION TIME 20 MINUTES
COOKING TIME 15 MINUTES

225g (8oz) [uncooked weight] basmati rice
1 large onion, finely chopped
2 garlic cloves, crushed
1 tsp ground cumin
1 tsp ground coriander
2 tsps ground cardamom
1 green chilli, sliced
450ml (¾ pint) vegetable stock
1 clove
1 tbsp runny honey
2 spring onions, chopped

1 Rinse the rice well under running water.
2 Dry-fry the onion and garlic in a preheated non-stick wok for
   1–2 minutes until soft. Add the spices, chilli and rice and
   continue cooking for 1 minute.
3 Add the stock, clove and honey and bring to the boil.
   Reduce the heat and simmer gently for 15 minutes until
   most of the liquid has been absorbed. Continue to cook over
   a very low heat until the rice is cooked. Stir in the spring
   onions and serve.

Tofu and pepper stir-fry with rice ⓥ

SERVES 4
1 SERVING 295 KCAL/2.9G FAT
PREPARATION TIME 10 MINUTES
COOKING TIME 10 MINUTES

225g (8oz) [uncooked weight] basmati rice
1 vegetable stock cube
1 × 349g pack Blue Dragon tofu
olive oil spray
1 medium red onion, finely sliced
2 garlic cloves, crushed
1 red pepper, seeded and diced
1 yellow pepper, seeded and diced
1 small red chilli, sliced
1 tsp finely chopped fresh ginger
1 tbsp light soy sauce
1 tbsp chopped fresh chives to garnish

1 Cook the rice in boiling water with the vegetable stock cube.
2 While the rice is cooking, drain the tofu and pat dry using
   kitchen paper. Cut into 16 pieces.
3 Heat a non-stick wok or frying pan. Spray with a little olive
   oil spray to prevent the tofu sticking. Add the tofu and cook
   lightly on both sides. Remove from the pan and keep warm.
4 Add the onion and garlic and cook until soft. Add the
   peppers, chilli, ginger and soy sauce. Cook quickly over a
   high heat until the peppers are just cooked.
5 Return the tofu to the pan and toss well.
6 Drain the rice. Serve with the tofu and pepper stir-fry with
   the rice and garnish with chopped chives.

Sweet potato, pepper and fennel bake Ⓥ

SERVES 4
1 SERVING 340 KCAL/4G FAT
PREPARATION TIME 30 MINUTES
COOKING TIME 55 MINUTES

675g (1½lb) sweet potatoes, cut into small dice
1 large bulb fennel, thinly sliced
2 red peppers, seeded and finely sliced
4 leeks, washed and sliced
2 garlic cloves, crushed
600ml (1 pint) skimmed milk
2 tsps vegetable bouillon powder
2 tbsps cornflour
50g (2oz) low-fat Cheddar cheese
2 tbsps chopped fresh chives
salt and freshly ground black pepper

1 Preheat the oven to 200C, 400F, Gas Mark 6.
2 Cook the sweet potatoes in boiling salted water. Drain well.
3 Dry-fry the fennel in a preheated non-stick pan until it starts to colour. Remove from pan and set aside.
4 Add the peppers, leeks and garlic to the pan and cook over a high heat until they start to colour.
5 Heat the milk and stock powder in a saucepan until boiling. Slake the cornflour with a little water and add to the milk, stirring continuously to prevent any lumps forming.
6 Mix in the cheese and chives and season with salt and black pepper.

7   In an ovenproof dish place alternate layers of potato, sauce and onion mixture, finishing with a layer of potato.
8   Bake in the oven for 20–25 minutes until brown and crisp.

Stir-fry Quorn Ⓥ

SERVES 4
1 SERVING 130 KCAL/4.8G FAT
PREPARATION TIME 15 MINUTES
COOKING TIME 10 MINUTES

olive oil spray
450g (1lb) Quorn chunks
2 tsps ground coriander
8 spring onions, chopped
115g (4oz) pak choi or spring greens
115g (4oz) mange-tout
2 medium carrots, cut into julienne strips
grated root ginger to taste
1–2 tsps soy sauce
juice of 1 lemon
salt and freshly ground black pepper

1   Spray a non-stick wok or pan lightly with olive oil spray. Add the Quorn, ground coriander and spring onions and cook for a few minutes.
2   Add the remaining vegetables and the grated ginger. Continue to cook until the Quorn and vegetables are cooked but the vegetables are still crunchy.
3   Add the soy sauce and lemon juice. Season to taste and serve immediately.

Bean and burgundy casserole ⓥ

SERVES 6
1 SERVING 326 KCAL/4G FAT
PREPARATION TIME 20 MINUTES
SOAKING TIME (LENTILS) 1 HOUR
COOKING TIME 45 MINUTES

175g (6oz) [uncooked weight] green lentils
1 tbsp vegetable oil
2 medium onions, finely chopped
2 garlic cloves, crushed
2 tsps cumin seeds
1 tsp dried oregano
300ml (½ pint) red wine
1 × 400g can chopped tomatoes
450–600ml (¾–1 pint) vegetable stock
1 bay leaf
450g (1lb) new potatoes, cut into large dice
1–2 large carrots, sliced
225g (8oz) leeks, cut into 2.5cm (1in) lengths
1 × 400g can red kidney beans, drained and rinsed
175–225g (6–8oz) small button mushrooms
1 small cauliflower, broken into florets (optional)
salt and freshly ground black pepper
1 tbsp chopped fresh parsley to garnish

1 Soak the lentils in cold water for at least an hour. Drain.
2 Heat the oil in a large pan and cook the onions gently until
   soft. Add the garlic, cumin seeds and oregano and cook for a
   further 2–3 minutes. Add the drained lentils, wine, tomatoes,
   450ml (¾ pint) of the vegetable stock and the bay leaf.

Bring to the boil, cover the pan and simmer for 10–15 minutes.

3 Add the potatoes, carrots, leeks and kidney beans to the pan. Bring back to the boil, adding more stock if necessary, and simmer for a further 10 minutes.

4 Add the mushrooms and cauliflower (if using) to the pan and continue cooking for a further 7–10 minutes or until the lentils are tender.

5 When the lentils are tender, remove the bay leaf from the pan and season the vegetables to taste with salt and pepper. Just before serving, pour the casserole into a hot serving dish and sprinkle the chopped parsley over the top.

Mediterranean stuffed peppers ⓥ

SERVES 4
1 SERVING 122 KCAL/3G FAT
PREPARATION TIME 15 MINUTES
COOKING TIME 35 MINUTES

These peppers can be made in advance and served cold or reheated and served hot.

2 red and 2 yellow peppers, seeded and cut in half
1 red onion, finely chopped
2 garlic cloves, crushed
2 medium courgettes, finely diced
115g (4oz) chestnut mushrooms, finely chopped
300ml (½ pint) tomato passata
2 tbsps chopped fresh basil
25g (1oz) grated Parmesan cheese
salt and freshly ground black pepper

1 Preheat the oven to 200C, 400F, Gas Mark 6.
2 Place the pepper shells on a non-stick baking tray and season with salt and black pepper.
3 In a preheated non-stick pan dry-fry the onion, garlic and courgettes for 5–6 minutes until they start to brown. Add the mushrooms and continue to cook over a high heat. Remove from the heat and stir in the tomato passata and chopped basil.
4 Pile the mixture into the pepper shells and top with the Parmesan cheese. Bake in the oven for 20–25 minutes until the peppers are cooked. Serve hot or cold.

Vegetable rice bake ⓥ

SERVES 4
1 SERVING 287 KCAL/7.6G FAT
PREPARATION TIME 30 MINUTES
COOKING TIME 30 MINUTES

1 tsp olive oil
1 small onion, sliced
1 red pepper, sliced
2 courgettes, sliced
1 small aubergine, cubed
225g (8oz) mushrooms, sliced
1 × 400g can chopped tomatoes with herbs
2 tbsps tomato purée
450g (1lb) cooked basmati rice
2 small eggs, beaten
1 tbsp sunflower seeds
salt and freshly ground black pepper

1 Preheat the oven to 180C, 350F, Gas Mark 4.
2 Heat the oil in a large pan and fry the onions for 3–4 minutes until softened. Add the red pepper, courgettes, aubergine and mushrooms to the pan and add 3 tbsps water. Cover and cook gently until the vegetables begin to soften. Stir in the tomatoes and tomato purée, bring to the boil and simmer for 10 minutes. Season to taste with salt and pepper. Pour into a shallow ovenproof dish.
3 Place the cooked rice in a mixing bowl, add the eggs and sunflower seeds. Season well and mix until combined. Spread over the tomato mixture and level the top.
4 Bake in the oven for 30 minutes until the top is golden brown.

Citrus rice pilaff Ⓥ ❄

SERVES 4
1 SERVING 176 KCAL/0.6G FAT
PREPARATION TIME 15 MINUTES
COOKING TIME 30 MINUTES

1 white onion, finely chopped
1 garlic clove, crushed
1 tsp crushed coriander seed
zest and juice of 1 lemon
good pinch of saffron
175g (6oz) [uncooked weight] basmati rice
450ml (¾ pint) vegetable stock
2 Thai lime leaves
black pepper
wedges of lemon and lime to garnish

1 Preheat a non-stick pan.
2 Add the onion and garlic and dry-fry until soft. Add the coriander seed and continue to cook for 2 minutes.
3 Add the lemon zest and juice, saffron, rice and stir in the stock. Bring to the boil, adding the Thai lime leaves.
4 Reduce the heat and cover with a lid. Simmer gently for 20 minutes until all the stock has been absorbed, add a little more if the mixture appears a little dry.
5 Once the rice is fully cooked add the lemon juice, season with fresh black pepper and stir well. Garnish with wedges of lemon and lime.

Butter bean hotpot ⓥ

SERVES 4
1 SERVING 330 KCAL/2.2G FAT
PREPARATION TIME 15 MINUTES
COOKING TIME 2 HOURS

225g (8oz) dried butter beans, soaked overnight
2 red onions, finely sliced
2 garlic cloves, crushed
4 rashers Quorn Deli slices, chopped
450g (1lb) potatoes, peeled and sliced
450g (1lb) cooking apples, peeled and sliced
2 fresh sage leaves
1 tbsp chopped fresh thyme
1 litre (1¾ pints) vegetable stock
freshly ground black pepper
2 tbsps chopped fresh parsley

1 Drain the beans and rinse well in cold water. Place in a
   saucepan and cover with cold water. Bring to the boil and
   boil for 10 minutes. Reduce the heat and simmer for 40
   minutes until tender. Drain.
2 Preheat the oven to 150C, 300F, Gas Mark 2.
3 In a preheated non-stick pan, dry-fry the onions and garlic
   for 2–3 minutes until soft. Add the Quorn Deli slices and
   season well with black pepper.
4 Lightly grease a casserole dish with Fry Light spray. Add a
   layer of potatoes, followed by the apples, beans and the
   onion mix, sprinkling the sage and thyme between each
   layer. Finish with a layer of potatoes.
5 Pour the stock over and cover. Bake in the centre of the oven
   for 1½–2 hours. Remove the cover and brown the potatoes
   for the last 20 minutes.
6 Sprinkle with parsley and serve hot.

Crunchy vegetable pasta ⓥ

SERVES 4
1 SERVING 280 KCAL/3.4G FAT
PREPARATION TIME 10 MINUTES
COOKING TIME 25 MINUTES

*This light and tasty pasta dish uses crisp young vegetables.
Adding a stock cube to the pasta water really makes a
difference. Save the stock for soups or freeze for later.*

225g (8oz) [uncooked weight] pasta shapes
1 vegetable stock cube
8 spring onions, finely chopped
1 garlic clove, crushed
150ml (¼ pint) white wine
115g (4oz) baby asparagus
115g (4oz) baby courgettes, cut into strips
115g (4oz) sugar snap peas
2 tbsps low-fat fromage frais
2 tbsps Parmesan cheese
freshly ground black pepper
1 tbsp chopped fresh mint to garnish

1 In a large saucepan cook the pasta in plenty of boiling water
   with the vegetable stock cube.
2 Preheat a non-stick pan, add the spring onions and garlic
   and dry-fry for 1–2 minutes until soft. Add the white wine
   and vegetables, and season with black pepper. Cook for 3–4
   minutes until the vegetables are just done.
3 Remove the pan from the heat and fold in the fromage frais
   and Parmesan cheese.
4 Drain the pasta into a warmed serving dish and spoon the
   vegetables over. Garnish with the mint and serve hot.

Hot and sour noodle stir-fry Ⓥ

SERVES 2
1 SERVING 304 KCAL/5.2G FAT
PREPARATION TIME 10 MINUTES
COOKING TIME 10 MINUTES

115g (4oz) [uncooked weight] fine noodles
1 vegetable stock cube
zest and juice of 1 lime
4 spring onions, finely sliced
2 garlic cloves, crushed
1 small red chilli, sliced
1 green pepper, seeded and sliced
4 small broccoli heads, sliced
115g (4oz) sugar snap peas
2 tsps finely chopped fresh ginger
1 tbsp light soy sauce
1 tbsp dry sherry
1 tbsp chopped fresh coriander to garnish

1 Cook the noodles in a pan of water with the vegetable stock
   cube. Drain and toss with the lime zest and juice.
2 Dry-fry the onion and garlic in a non-stick wok or frying pan
   until soft. Add the green pepper, broccoli, sugar snap peas,
   ginger and soy sauce. Cook quickly over a high heat until the
   vegetables are just cooked.
3 Add the sherry, and toss well.
4 Add the noodles and mix well.
5 Serve in warmed bowls and sprinkle with chopped coriander.

Spicy chickpea casserole Ⓥ

SERVES 4
1 SERVING 160 KCAL/3.8G FAT
PREPARATION TIME 25 MINUTES
COOKING TIME 40 MINUTES

2 medium leeks, finely chopped
2 courgettes, diced
3 celery sticks, chopped
½ tsp ground cumin
½ tsp ground turmeric
½ tsp ground five spice
2 garlic cloves, chopped
2 tsps chopped fresh oregano
1 × 400g can chickpeas
600ml (1 pint) vegetable stock
2 tsps cornflour
freshly ground black pepper
2 pieces fresh orange peel, finely shredded
courgette strips to garnish

1 Place the prepared leeks, courgettes and celery in a
   preheated non-stick pan and dry-fry for 2–3 minutes until
   lightly coloured.
2 Add the spices, garlic and oregano and continue to cook for
   1 minute.
3 Rinse the chickpeas under cold running water, and add to
   the pan.
4 Add the stock and bring the mixture to a gentle simmer.
5 Mix the cornflour in a small bowl with a little cold water to a
   smooth paste.

6 Stir the slaked cornflour into the casserole and simmer gently for 5 minutes.
7 Garnish with the finely shredded orange peel and some finely shredded courgette strips.

Roast vegetable and tomato pasta ⓥ

1 SERVING 245 KCAL/1.5G FAT
PREPARATION TIME 20 MINUTES
COOKING TIME 30 MINUTES

1 red and 1 yellow pepper, seeded
1 red onion, peeled
1 courgette
6 chestnut mushrooms, cut into quarters
1 garlic clove, sliced
2 tsps ground coriander
1 tbsp low-salt soy sauce
1 tbsp chopped fresh herbs (coriander, chives, parsley)
300ml (½ pint) tomato passata
225g (8oz) [uncooked weight] pasta shapes
1 vegetable stock cube
freshly ground black pepper

1 Preheat the oven to 190C, 375F, Gas Mark 5.
2 Chop the peppers, onion and courgette into bite-sized pieces and place in a non-stick roasting tray. Add the mushrooms and garlic.
3 Sprinkle the ground coriander over, season to taste, and drizzle with the soy sauce.
4 Place in the top of the oven and roast for 20-25 minutes.

5 When cooked, spoon into a saucepan, add the passata and
   herbs and place over a low heat to heat through.
6 Cook the pasta in boiling water with the vegetable stock.
   Drain and place in 4 serving bowls. Spoon the sauce over.

Aubergine sombrero pasta Ⓥ

SERVES 4
1 SERVING 260 KCAL/1.2G FAT
PREPARATION TIME 10 MINUTES
COOKING TIME 25 MINUTES

225g (8oz) [uncooked weight] pasta shapes
1 vegetable stock cube
1 small red onion, finely chopped
2 smoked garlic cloves, crushed
1 small aubergine
1 red pepper, finely diced
2 baby courgettes, finely diced
pinch of sweet paprika
1 small red chilli, finely chopped
1 × 400g can chopped tomatoes
2 tbsps chopped fresh parsley to garnish

1 Cook the pasta in a large saucepan of boiling water with the
   stock cube.
2 In a preheated non-stick pan dry-fry the onion until soft.
   Add the garlic and aubergine and continue cooking for 2–3
   minutes. Add the remaining ingredients, except the parsley,
   and simmer gently for 5–6 minutes.
3 Drain the pasta thoroughly, arrange on warmed plates and
   serve with sauce on top. Garnish with chopped fresh parsley.

Lentil roast ⓥ

SERVES 4
1 SERVING 377 KCAL/1.9G FAT
PREPARATION TIME 20 MINUTES,
COOKING TIME 1 HOUR

*This creamy tomato lentil roast with a crunchy topping can be
eaten cold with salad.*

350g (12oz) orange lentils
1 bay leaf
2–3 parsley stalks
1 sprig fresh thyme
2 large onions, chopped
1-2 garlic cloves, crushed
1 tsp ground cumin
2–3 celery sticks, sliced
1 vegetable stock cube
1 dessert apple
½ green pepper, seeded and diced
½ red pepper, seeded and diced
1 × 400g can chopped tomatoes
75g (3oz) Quark or low-fat natural yogurt
salt and freshly ground black pepper

1 Preheat the oven to 180C, 350F, Gas Mark 4.
2 Wash the lentils well, drain and place in a large pan. Cover
   with water.
3 Tie the bay leaf, parsley stalks and thyme together with
   string and add to the pan. Bring to the boil.

4 Add the onions, garlic, cumin and celery to the lentils, along with the stock cube, and simmer until the lentils and vegetables are tender and the liquid has almost evaporated.

5 Meanwhile, peel the apple, cut into quarters and remove the core. Cut the quarters into small dice.

6 When the lentils are tender, remove the bunch of herbs and continue cooking, stirring all the time until the mixture is quite dry.

7 Stir the diced apple, peppers, tomatoes and Quark or yogurt into the lentil mixture. Mix well and season to taste with salt and black pepper.

8 Pile the mixture into an ovenproof dish and bake in the oven for about 1 hour until the top is springy like a sponge.

Tomato and lemon penne Ⓥ

SERVES 4
1 SERVING 266 KCAL/3.9G FAT
PREPARATION TIME 20 MINUTES
COOKING TIME 30 MINUTES

225g (8oz) [uncooked weight] penne pasta
1 vegetable stock cube
1 red onion, finely chopped
2 garlic cloves, crushed
1 red pepper, seeded and finely sliced
1 × 400g can chopped tomatoes
1 red chilli, seeded and finely sliced
zest of 1 lemon
8–10 basil leaves, shredded
salt and freshly ground black pepper
lemon segments to garnish

1 Cook the pasta in boiling water with a vegetable stock cube. Meanwhile, preheat a non-stick frying pan, add the onion and dry-fry for 2–3 minutes until soft. Add the garlic and red pepper and cook for 2–3 minutes more. Add the tomatoes, chilli and lemon zest and bring the sauce to a gentle simmer. Season to taste with freshly ground black pepper.
2 Drain the pasta and pour into a serving dish.
3 Spoon the sauce over the pasta and sprinkle the shredded basil on top. Serve garnished with the lemon segments.

Creamy basil pasta ⓥ

SERVES 4
1 SERVING 227 KCAL/2.2G FAT
PREPARATION TIME 20 MINUTES
COOKING TIME 15 MINUTES

This low-fat pesto is a really tasty light sauce for all types of pasta. It can be made in advance and stored in the refrigerator for up to a week.

225g (8oz) [uncooked weight] penne pasta
2 vegetable stock cubes
2 good bunches fresh basil
1 garlic clove, crushed
2 tbsps virtually fat-free fromage frais
1 tbsp grated fresh Parmesan cheese
freshly ground black pepper

1 Cook the pasta in boiling water with 1 vegetable stock cube.
2 Meanwhile, in a small saucepan, dissolve the other vegetable stock cube in 150ml (¼ pint) of boiling water.

3   Remove the leaves from the basil and place in a food
    processor or liquidiser with the garlic and hot vegetable
    stock. Blend until smooth to form a pesto.
4   Drain the pasta and return to the hot pan. Add the pesto and
    fromage frais, mixing well. Season well with black pepper.
5   Pour into a serving dish and sprinkle with Parmesan cheese.

Butternut squash lasagne Ⓥ

SERVES 4
1 SERVING 416 KCAL/6G FAT
PREPARATION TIME 20 MINUTES
COOKING TIME 45 MINUTES

1 butternut squash
1 tbsp light soy sauce
1 large onion, finely diced
2 garlic cloves, crushed
1 × 400g can chopped tomatoes
300ml (½ pint) tomato passata
1 tbsp chopped fresh oregano or marjoram
8 lasagne pasta sheets
freshly ground black pepper

for the white sauce topping
600ml (1 pint) semi-skimmed milk
2 tbsps cornflour
2 tsps Dijon mustard
¼ tsp vegetable stock powder
2 tbsps grated Parmesan cheese
freshly ground black pepper

1 Preheat the oven to 200C, 400F, Gas Mark 6.

2 Cut the squash into quarters, using a sharp chopping knife. Remove the centre seeds and peel away the skin. Cut the flesh into large dice and place in a non-stick roasting tray. Drizzle with the soy sauce and place in the oven for 20 minutes until soft.

3 Dry-fry the onion in a non-stick pan until soft, add the garlic and cook for 1–2 minutes more. Add the chopped tomatoes, tomato passata, herbs and squash. Season with black pepper and simmer for 10 minutes.

4 Make the white sauce by heating the milk in a small saucepan. Mix the cornflour with a little cold milk and mix into the hot milk, stirring well to prevent any lumps forming. Stir in the mustard and stock powder and season with black pepper.

5 Place 2–3 tbsps of white sauce in the base of an ovenproof dish. Cover with a layer of lasagne sheets, then half the tomato sauce. Repeat with another layer of pasta and the remaining tomato sauce and finish with a layer of pasta. Pour the remaining white sauce on top and sprinkle with a little grated Parmesan cheese.

6 Bake in the oven for 25–30 minutes.

Aubergine and chickpea curry ⓥ

SERVES 4
1 SERVING 211 KCAL/4.4G FAT
PREPARATION TIME 20 MINUTES
COOKING TIME 35 MINUTES

This rich tomato-based curry benefits from being made a day in advance. For a creamy curry remove from the heat and stir in 2 tbsps virtually fat free fromage frais.

2 red onions, finely chopped
2 garlic cloves, crushed
1 large aubergine, diced
2 tsps chopped fresh thyme
½ tsp allspice
2 tsps ground cumin
1 tsp ground turmeric
1 tbsp chopped fresh ginger
2 red chillies, finely sliced
150ml (¼ pint) vegetable stock
1 tbsp plain flour
1 × 400g can chickpeas, drained
1 × 400g can chopped tomatoes
450ml (¾ pint) tomato passata

1 Preheat a non-stick pan. Add the onions, garlic and aubergine and dry-fry for 5 minutes until soft. Add the thyme and spices and cook for a further 2 minutes.
2 Add 3 tbsps of stock then stir in the flour and 'cook it out' over a low heat.

3 Gradually stir in the remaining stock, the chickpeas, chopped
   tomatoes and tomato passata. Simmer gently for 20 minutes
   to allow the sauce to thicken.

Quorn red Thai curry ⓥ

SERVES 4
1 SERVING 194 KCAL/7.2G FAT
PREPARATION TIME 10 MINUTES
COOKING TIME 20 MINUTES

1 large red onion, finely chopped
2 garlic cloves, crushed
250g (10oz) fresh or frozen Quorn pieces
1 tsp ground coriander
1 tsp finely chopped lemongrass
1 red pepper, finely sliced
600ml (1 pint) tomato passata
1 small red chilli, finely sliced
1 Kaffir lime leaf
freshly ground black pepper
1 tbsp chopped fresh coriander

1 Preheat a non-stick wok or frying pan.
2 Add the onion and garlic and dry-fry for 2–3 minutes until
   soft. Add the Quorn pieces and season well with salt and
   black pepper. Stir in the ground coriander and the
   lemongrass. Add the remaining ingredients and bring to a
   gentle simmer. Reduce the heat and allow to simmer for 10
   minutes until the sauce has reduced slightly.
3 Just before serving, garnish with chopped coriander.

Sweet and sour vegetable tofu ⓥ

SERVES 2
1 SERVING 246 KCAL/8G FAT
PREPARATION TIME 10 MINUTES
COOKING TIME 15 MINUTES

for the marinade
1 tbsp reduced-salt soy sauce
1 tbsp sherry
1 small chilli, finely sliced
1 garlic clove, crushed
225g (8oz) tofu

1 medium red onion, finely sliced
1 courgette, sliced
1 red pepper, seeded and diced
2–3 chestnut mushrooms, sliced
1 tbsp balsamic vinegar
1 tbsp runny honey
50g (2oz) mange-tout, sliced
1 tbsp chopped fresh coriander
freshly ground black pepper

1 Mix together the marinade ingredients in a small bowl.
2 Dice the tofu, add to the marinade, and mix well.
3 Preheat a non-stick wok. Add the onion, courgette, red pepper and mushrooms, and dry-fry for 6–7 minutes until they start to colour.
4 Add the tofu and the marinade and continue cooking, tossing the ingredients well to mix.

5 Add the balsamic vinegar and the honey, and simmer gently
   for 2–3 minutes. Finally stir in the mange-tout and coriander.
   Serve straight from the wok.

Vegetable chilli ⓥ ❄

SERVES: 4
1 SERVING 187 KCAL/1.4G FAT
PREPARATION TIME 30 MINUTES
COOKING TIME 1 HOUR

1 × 400g can chopped tomatoes
1 × 225g can red kidney beans, washed and drained
1 tsp tomato purée
2 tsps oil-free sweet pickle
1 garlic clove, crushed
1 eating apple, peeled, cored and chopped
1 onion, chopped
115g (4oz) broad beans
115g (4oz) peas
115g (4oz) carrots, chopped
115g (4oz) potatoes, chopped
1 tsp chilli powder
3 chillies, seeded and finely chopped
120ml (4fl oz) vegetable stock
1 bay leaf

1 Place all the ingredients in a saucepan and cover with a lid.
   Simmer for 1 hour over a low heat, stirring occasionally.
2 Remove the lid and continue to cook until the liquid is
   reduced and the mixture is of a thick consistency.

Red beans and rice ⓥ ❋

SERVES 4
1 SERVING 254 KCAL/2.2G FAT
PREPARATION TIME 15 MINUTES
COOKING TIME APPROX 25 MINUTES

2 medium onions, chopped
2 garlic cloves, crushed
115g (4oz) [uncooked weight] basmati rice
4 celery sticks, chopped
½ fennel bulb, chopped
300ml (½ pint) vegetable stock
1 × 400g can kidney beans, drained
1 × 400g can chopped tomatoes
½ tsp cayenne pepper
2 tbsps tomato purée
2 tsps chopped fresh thyme
salt and freshly ground black pepper
low-fat natural yogurt to serve

1 In a non-stick pan, dry-fry the onions and garlic until soft.
  Add the rice, celery and fennel and stir in the stock.
2 Add the drained kidney beans, tomatoes, cayenne pepper,
  tomato purée and thyme. Season with salt and black pepper.
3 Cover and simmer gently for 20 minutes. Remove the lid and
  stir well. Continue cooking until all the liquid is absorbed.
4 To serve, spoon into bowls, and drizzle a little low-fat natural
  yogurt on top.

Tomato and pepper pasta Ⓥ

SERVES 4
1 SERVING 234 KCAL/2G FAT
PREPARATION TIME 15 MINUTES
COOKING TIME APPROX 25 MINUTES

for the sauce
1 onion, chopped
1 garlic clove, crushed
2 × 400g cans chopped tomatoes
2½ tbsps white wine vinegar or cider vinegar
2 tbsps tomato ketchup or purée
1 tbsp soy sauce
2 bay leaves
1 tsp chopped fresh basil
1 tsp dried oregano
2 bay leaves
salt and freshly ground black pepper

for the pasta
200g (7oz) [uncooked weight] pasta shells or similar
1 vegetable stock cube
½ green pepper, seeded and chopped
½ red pepper, seeded and chopped
6 small mushrooms, sliced

1 Preheat a non-stick pan. Add the onion and dry-fry until
   soft, then add the crushed garlic. Add the remaining sauce
   ingredients and bring to the boil. Cover and simmer for 20
   minutes.

2 Remove the bay leaves, then transfer the mixture to a blender and purée for a few seconds.
3 Meanwhile, cook the pasta shells with the vegetable stock cube in boiling water for 12 minutes until just cooked. Drain and keep warm.
4 Add the chopped red and green peppers and sliced mushrooms to the sauce and cook for 1 minute before stirring in the cooked pasta. Serve immediately.

Lentil and potato pie Ⓥ

SERVES 3
1 SERVING 339 KCAL/1.2G FAT
PREPARATION TIME 20 MINUTES
COOKING TIME 1 HOUR

175g (6oz) red lentils, soaked overnight
1 large onion, chopped
350g (12oz) new potatoes
2 tbsps pickle
1 tsp mixed herbs
salt and freshly ground black pepper
paprika

1 Preheat the oven to 200C, 400F, Gas Mark 6.
2 Rinse the lentils and place with the onion in a pan. Cover with water and cook slowly for 20 minutes or until the lentils are tender and all the water is absorbed.
3 Cook the potatoes in boiling salted water, then drain and mash. Beat the mashed potato into the lentils. Add the mixed herbs, the pickle, a little salt and plenty of black pepper and mix well.

4 Place in a shallow ovenproof dish. Fork the top and sprinkle
   a little paprika over. Bake in the oven for 20 minutes until
   crisp and brown.

Saffron risotto ⓥ

SERVES 6
1 SERVING 189 KCAL/0.7G FAT
PREPARATION TIME 10 MINUTES
COOKING TIME 10 MINUTES

1 small white onion, finely chopped
300g (11oz) [uncooked weight] basmati rice
good pinch of saffron
1 litre (1¾ pints) vegetable stock
salt and freshly ground black pepper

1 Dry-fry the onion in a non-stick pan on a low heat for 3–4
   minutes or until soft without colour, then add the risotto
   rice.
2 Infuse the saffron with a little hot water and pour into the
   risotto. Start adding the vegetable stock, ladle by ladle,
   stirring constantly. Allow each ladle of stock to be absorbed
   by the rice before adding the next ladle. Cook, still stirring
   constantly, until the rice is al dente, usually about 20
   minutes. Season to taste.
3 Serve in a warmed bowl and sprinkle with a little saffron.

Summer vegetable bake ⓥ

SERVES 4
1 SERVING 237 KCAL/6G FAT
PREPARATION TIME 10 MINUTES
COOKING TIME 30 MINUTES

225g (8oz) baby carrots, chopped
1 vegetable stock cube
4 baby leeks, chopped
225g (8oz) small broccoli florets
2 small courgettes cut into sticks
115g (4oz) small chestnut mushrooms
600ml (1 pint) skimmed milk
2 tbsps cornflour
1 tbsp grain mustard
115g (4oz) low-fat Cheddar cheese
1 tbsp chopped fresh chives

1 Preheat the oven to 190C, 375F, Gas Mark 5.
2 Place the carrots and stock cube in a small saucepan. Cover
   with water and boil for 4–5 minutes.
3 Add the leeks, broccoli and courgettes and continue to cook
   for 2–3 minutes until the broccoli is just cooked. Remove
   from the heat, drain through a colander and place in the
   bottom of an ovenproof dish. Add the mushrooms.
4 Pour the milk into the pan and heat. Slake the cornflour with
   a little cold water and mix into the milk. Bring to the boil,
   stirring continuously. Remove from the heat and stir in the
   mustard, cheese and chives.
5 Pour the sauce over the vegetables and place in the oven for
   20 minutes until golden brown.

Peppers stuffed with wild mushrooms Ⓥ

SERVES 4
1 SERVING 46 KCAL/0.5G FAT
PREPARATION TIME 10 MINUTES
COOKING TIME 30 MINUTES

2 yellow peppers
225g (8oz) fresh wild mushrooms
2 long shallots, finely chopped
1 garlic clove, crushed
2 tsps chopped fresh thyme
1 tbsp lemon juice
1 tsp ground coriander
1 tbsp chopped fresh parsley
2 tbsps virtually fat free fromage frais
salt and freshly ground black pepper

1 Preheat the oven to 200C, 400F, Gas Mark 6.
2 Cut the peppers in half, remove the seeds and discard. Place the pepper halves on a non-stick baking tray and bake in the oven for 15–20 minutes until they start to soften.
3 Slice the wild mushrooms and rinse in a colander.
4 In a non-stick pan, dry-fry the shallots and garlic until soft. Add the thyme and mushrooms, and cook quickly for 1–2 minutes. Add the lemon juice, coriander and parsley and mix well.
5 Remove from the heat and fold in the fromage frais. Fill each pepper half with the mushroom mix and return to the oven for 5–6 minutes to heat through. Serve warm.

Creamy lemon broad beans ⓥ

SERVES 4
1 SERVING 125 KCAL/1.5G FAT
PREPARATION TIME 10 MINUTES
COOKING TIME 20 MINUTES

Pep up broad beans with this creamy lemon dressing. Baby broad beans tend to be much sweeter in flavour and have softer skins than the larger ones.

500g (1¼lb) frozen baby broad beans
8 spring onions, sliced
zest and juice of 1 lemon
grated fresh nutmeg
3 tbsps low-fat Greek-style yogurt
freshly ground black pepper

1   Cook the broad beans in a pan of lightly salted water. Drain well and return to the saucepan. Add the lemon and yogurt and mix well.
2   Season well with black pepper and grated fresh nutmeg. Pile into a warm serving dish and serve.

Sautéed courgettes and cherry tomatoes Ⓥ

SERVES 4
1 SERVING 22 KCAL/0.5G FAT
PREPARATION TIME 10 MINUTES
COOKING TIME 20 MINUTES

Choose small young courgettes with a shiny bloom. Old courgettes become tough and withered and have a strong bitter flavour.

225g (8oz) courgettes, sliced
225g (8oz) cherry tomatoes, cut in half
1 garlic clove, crushed
pinch of sea salt
freshly ground black pepper
a few basil leaves to garnish

1 Preheat a non-stick frying pan. Add the courgettes and the garlic and dry-fry over a moderate heat for 5–6 minutes until soft. Season with salt and black pepper.
2 Add the tomatoes and continue cooking for 1–2 minutes to heat through. Just before serving sprinkle with fresh basil.

Roast sweet potatoes with chilli glaze ⓥ

SERVES 4
1 SERVING 124 KCAL/0.5G FAT
PREPARATION TIME 10 MINUTES
COOKING TIME 35 MINUTES

450g (1lb) sweet potatoes
1 vegetable stock cube
1 medium red onion, finely diced
2 tbsps light soy sauce
1 tsp sea salt
1 red chilli, seeded and finely chopped
1 garlic clove, crushed
2 tbsps apple sauce
1 tbsp chopped fresh parsley

1 Preheat the oven to 200C, 400F, Gas Mark 6.
2 Wash the potatoes and cut into 2.5cm (1in) pieces. Cook in a
   pan of boiling water with a vegetable stock cube for 5
   minutes then drain well.
3 Place the potatoes in the bottom of a non-stick baking tin.
   Add the red onion. Drizzle the soy sauce over and sprinkle
   with salt. Bake in the oven for 20–25 minutes.
4 Remove from the oven. Combine the chilli, garlic and apple
   sauce and dot over the potatoes. Shake the tin well to coat
   the potatoes then return to the oven for 5 minutes. Just
   before serving sprinkle with parsley.

Dressings

Balsamic dressing Ⓥ

MAKES 180ML (6½FL OZ)
1 TBSP 12 KCAL/0.2G FAT
PREPARATION TIME 5 MINUTES

150ml (1¼ pint) apple juice
2 tbsps balsamic vinegar
1 tbsp Dijon mustard
pinch of sugar
salt and freshly ground black pepper

1 Combine all the ingredients in a small bowl and whisk until
   smooth.
2 Place in a jar or bottle and seal the top. Use within 5 days.

Fat-free mayonnaise Ⓥ

MAKES 220ML (7½FL OZ))
1 TBSP 9 KCAL/0.02G FAT
PREPARATION TIME 5 MINUTES

175g (6oz) virtually fat free fromage-frais
2 tbsps cider vinegar
1 tbsp lemon juice
¼ tsp ground turmeric
2 tsps sugar
salt and freshly ground black pepper

1 Combine all the ingredients in a small bowl and whisk until smooth.
2 Place in a container, seal the top, and store in the refrigerator. Use within 3 days.

Honey and orange dressing ⓥ

MAKES 150ML (¼ PINT)
1 TBSP 11 KCAL/0.02G FAT
PREPARATION TIME 10 MINUTES
COOKING TIME 5 MINUTES

6 tbsps fresh orange juice
4 tsps runny honey
1 tbsp white wine vinegar
½ tsp Dijon wholegrain mustard
1 tsp grated orange rind
2 tsps chopped fresh chives and parsley (mixed)
salt and freshly ground black pepper to taste

1 Place the orange juice, honey and vinegar in a pan. Add the Dijon mustard and orange rind. Bring to the boil, and allow to cool.
2 When cool, add the chopped chives and parsley and season to taste with salt and black pepper. Place in a bottle or jar, seal the top and place in the refrigerator. Use within 7 days.

Oil-free vinaigrette ⓥ

MAKES 200ML (7FL OZ)
1 TBSP 9 KCAL/0.1G FAT
PREPARATION TIME 5 MINUTES

150ml (¼ pint) white wine vinegar or cider vinegar
50ml (2fl oz) lemon juice
3–4 tsps caster sugar
1½ tsps French mustard
chopped fresh herbs, e.g. marjoram, basil or parsley (optional)
1 garlic clove, crushed (optional)
½ tsp salt
½ tsp freshly ground black pepper

1 Combine all the ingredients and pour into a screw top jar or other container that has a tight-fitting lid. Shake well. Taste and add more salt, pepper or sugar if you wish.
2 Seal the top and store in the refrigerator. Shake well before using.

Garlic and yogurt dressing Ⓥ

SERVES 4
1 SERVING 20 KCAL/0.3G FAT
PREPARATION TIME 5 MINUTES

1 garlic clove, crushed
150g (5oz) low-fat natural yogurt
1 tbsp wine vinegar
1 tsp reduced-oil salad dressing
salt and freshly ground black pepper to taste

1 Combine all the ingredients in a container and shake well.
   Taste and add more salt or sugar as desired.
2 Seal the top and store in the refrigerator.

Marie Rose dressing Ⓥ

SERVES 2
1 SERVING 73 KCAL/1G FAT
PREPARATION TIME 5 MINUTES

2 tbsps tomato ketchup
1 tbsp reduced-oil salad dressing
4 tbsps low-fat natural yogurt
dash of Tabasco sauce
salt and freshly ground black pepper to taste

1 Combine all the ingredients in a jar or other container.
2 Seal the top and store in the refrigerator. Use within 2 days.

Oil-free orange and lemon vinaigrette dressing ⓥ

SERVES 4
1 SERVING 7 KCAL/0.08GFAT
PREPARATION TIME 5 MINUTES

4 tbsps wine vinegar
4 tbsps lemon juice
4 tbsps orange juice
grated rind of 1 lemon
½ tsp French mustard
pinch of garlic salt
freshly ground black pepper

1 Place all the ingredients in a bowl and mix thoroughly.
2 Transfer to a container or jar and seal tightly. Keep in the refrigerator and use within 2 days.

Desserts

Rhubarb and apple fool ⓥ

SERVES 4
1 SERVING 200 KCAL/0.1G FAT
PREPARATION TIME 15 MINUTES
COOKING TIME 20 MINUTES

Choose thin, brightly coloured rhubarb sticks with more red rouge colour than green. The greener the stems, the more bitter the flavour.

225g (8oz) rhubarb
225g (8oz) cooking apples
115g (4oz) caster sugar
2 tbsps whisky or brandy
225g (8oz) Quark (low-fat soft cheese)
2 egg whites
fresh mint to decorate

1 Wash and trim the rhubarb, then chop into small pieces and place in a saucepan.
2 Peel, core and slice the apples and add to the pan.
3 Cook the rhubarb over a low heat until soft, stirring from time to time to prevent the fruit from sticking.
4 Add the sugar and reduce to a thick purée. Allow to cool. Beat in the Quark to a smooth consistency.
5 Whisk the egg whites until they stand in stiff peaks. Using a metal spoon, gently fold the egg whites into the fruit purée and sweeten to taste with extra sugar.
6 Spoon into individual glasses and decorate with fresh mint.

Blackberry and port ice ⓥ

SERVES 4
1 SERVING 108 KCAL/0.2G FAT
PREPARATION TIME 15 MINUTES
COOKING TIME 10 MINUTES
FREEZING TIME 12 HOURS

50g (2oz) caster sugar
450g (1lb) blackberries
zest and juice of 2 oranges
2 tbsps white port
1 egg white
fresh fruit to decorate

1 In a small saucepan dissolve the sugar in 300ml (½ pint) water and bring to the boil. Remove from the heat and allow to cool.
2 Rinse the blackberries under cold water and place in a food processor with the orange zest, juice and port. Blend until smooth.
3 Mix the fruit purée with the cooled syrup and pass through a fine sieve into a shallow freezer container. Cover and freeze for 3 hours until mushy. Remove from the freezer and break up with a fork.
4 Whisk the egg white until stiff. Fold into the loosened mixture and return to the freezer until firm, ideally overnight.
5 Twenty minutes before serving, remove from the freezer and place in the refrigerator to allow it to soften slightly.
6 Just before serving, decorate with fresh fruit.

Moroccan clementines (V)

1 SERVING 80 KCAL/0.2G FAT
PREPARATION TIME 5 MINUTES
COOKING TIME 2–3 MINUTES

4 clementines
1 tsp ground ginger
1 tsp ground cinnamon
2 tsps demerara sugar
4 tbsps virtually fat free fromage frais
mint to decorate

1 Preheat the grill to high. Using a sharp knife, slice the
   clementines in half across the centres and place on a baking
   tray lined with aluminium foil.
2 Sprinkle the spices and the demerara sugar on top and place
   the clementines under the grill. Cook for 2–3 minutes until
   golden brown.
3 Decorate with mint and serve hot with the fromage frais.

Strawberries with black pepper and balsamic dressing (V)

SERVES 4
1 SERVING 60 KCAL/0.1G FAT
PREPARATION TIME 10 MINUTES
COOKING TIME 5 MINUTES

*It's best to assemble this dessert just before required, although
you can prepare the strawberries in advance and store in the
refrigerator.*

450g (1lb) fresh strawberries, hulled
good pinch of cracked black pepper
2 tbsps dry sherry
1 tbsp good quality balsamic vinegar
zest of 1 lime
1 tbsp icing sugar
300ml (½ pint) 0% fat Greek-style yogurt

1 Using a small knife, cut the strawberries in half, place in a
   serving dish and sprinkle with the cracked black pepper.
2 In a small bowl mix together the sherry and the balsamic
   vinegar. Pour over the strawberries. Sprinkle with the lime
   zest and dust with the icing sugar. Serve with the yogurt.

Strawberry dream ⓥ

SERVES 4
1 SERVING 99 KCAL/1.4G FAT
PREPARATION TIME 15 MINUTES
COOKING TIME 10 MINUTES

225g (8oz) fresh strawberries, hulled
1 × 75g packet instant low-fat custard powder
300ml (½ pint) skimmed milk
300g (11oz) low-fat Greek yogurt
2 tsps sugar
2 egg whites
mint leaves to decorate

1 Using a fork, mash the strawberries well and set aside.
2 Make up the custard according to the packet instructions.

3 Stir in the strawberries, cover with food wrap and allow to cool.
4 Once cold, beat the yogurt into the custard mixture and sweeten to taste with a little sugar.
5 Whisk the egg whites to stiff peaks and gently fold into the mixture.
6 Spoon into individual glasses and decorate with mint leaves.

Cardamom and orange rice pudding ⓥ

SERVES 6
1 SERVING 83 KCAL/0.2G FAT
PREPARATION TIME 5 MINUTES
COOKING TIME 35 MINUTES

65g (2¼oz) flaked rice
600ml (1 pint) skimmed milk
1 tbsp caster sugar
zest and juice of 1 orange
8 cardamom pods

1 Place the flaked rice, milk, sugar and orange in a saucepan. Bring to the boil, then reduce the heat to a gentle simmer.
2 Place the cardamom pods on a chopping board and crush, using the broad edge of a knife. Carefully tease out the seeds and add them to the rice. Discard the pods.
3 Cover with a lid and cook for 30–35 minutes, stirring occasionally. Alternatively, place all the ingredients in a large bowl, cover and microwave on full power for 10 minutes, stir well and return for a further 10 minutes. Adjust the consistency with a little extra milk.
4 Serve hot with a little virtually fat free fromage frais.

Chocolate orange cups ⓥ

SERVES 6
1 SERVING 106 KCAL/4G FAT
PREPARATION TIME 5 MINUTES
COOKING TIME 10 MINUTES

1 × 75g (3oz) packet instant chocolate custard
2 tsps bitter cocoa powder (Valrhona or Green & Black's)
1 orange
1 tbsp caster sugar
6 dark chocolate cups
mint to decorate

1 Make up the custard according to the packet instructions,
   stir in the cocoa and allow to cool.
2 Slice the orange in half lengthways, then slice down to give
   semi-circles. Place the orange pieces in a small saucepan and
   just cover with boiling water. Add the sugar and simmer over
   a low heat for 10 minutes until soft. Remove from the heat
   and allow to cool.
3 Assemble the desserts by filling the cups with the cold
   custard, then top with 2 slices of orange. Place a third
   twisted slice of orange on top and decorate with fresh mint.
   Chill until required.

Cranberry and orange granita sorbet Ⓥ ❄

SERVES 4
1 SERVING 81 KCAL/0.06G FAT
PREPARATION TIME 15 MINUTES
COOKING TIME 10 MINUTES
FREEZING TIME 12 HOURS

If you wish, you can omit the alcohol or substitute a cordial such as elderflower. As the egg is not cooked make sure it is very fresh.

50g (2oz) low-calorie granulated sugar
225g (8oz) fresh or frozen cranberries
zest and juice of 2 oranges
2 tbsps vodka
1 very fresh egg white
fresh fruit to decorate

1 In a medium saucepan dissolve the sugar in 300ml (½ pint) water, add the cranberries and bring to the boil. Simmer gently until the cranberries have all split and appear soft. Remove from the heat and stir. Allow to cool.
2 Place in a food processor with the orange zest, juice and vodka and blend until smooth. Pour into a shallow freezer container. Cover and freeze for 3 hours until mushy. Remove from the freezer and break up with a fork.
3 Whisk the egg white until stiff. Fold into the loosened mixture and return to the freezer until firm, ideally overnight.

4 Twenty minutes before serving remove from the freezer and
   place in the refrigerator to allow it soften slightly.
5 Serve in frosted glasses and decorate with fresh fruit.

Apricot and cherry filo stack ⓥ

SERVES 4
1 SERVING 158 KCAL/0.4G FAT
PREPARATION TIME 10 MINUTES
COOKING TIME 15 MINUTES

*An easy but stylish way to serve fresh fruit. Make the wafers in
advance and store in an airtight tin.*

4 sheets filo pastry
1 egg beaten with 1 tbsp skimmed milk
1 tbsp caster sugar
4 ripe apricots
175g (6oz) ripe cherries
300g (11oz) 0% fat Greek yogurt
fresh mint to decorate
icing sugar to dust

1 Preheat the oven to 200C, 400F, Gas Mark 6.
2 Place a sheet of filo pastry on a chopping board. Brush well
   with the beaten egg, then cover with a second sheet of
   pastry. Repeat the process until all the sheets are used. Brush
   the top layer and sprinkle with sugar.
3 Using a large chopping knife, cut the pastry into 8 equal
   squares. Transfer the squares to a non-stick baking tray and
   bake in the oven for 8–10 minutes until golden brown. Allow
   to cool.

4 Remove the stones from the apricots and cherries. Cut the apricots into small wedges.

5 Assemble the dessert by layering a quarter of the fuit and yogurt between 2 filo wafers. Repeat with the remaining fruit and pastry. Decorate with mint and dust with a little icing sugar.

Cosmopolitan cocktail Ⓥ

SERVES 4
1 SERVING 75 KCAL/0.4G FAT
PREPARATION TIME 5 MINUTES

A delicious combination of soft fruits spiked with passion fruit. Prepare in advance and serve chilled.

½ small melon
1 papaya
2 kiwi fruits
2 passion fruits

1 Prepare the melon by removing the outer skin with a sharp knife. Cut the flesh into small slices and place in a bowl.

2 Cut the papaya in half lengthways, scoop out the seeds with a spoon and discard. Peel away the outer skin and chop the flesh into small dice. Place in the bowl.

3 Top and tail the kiwi fruits, peel and cut into small dice. Place in the bowl.

4 Cut the passion fruit in half and, using a tsp, scoop out the seeds. Add to the bowl. Mix well.

5 Spoon the fruit cocktail into four serving glasses. Chill until ready to serve.

Fresh lime cheesecake

SERVES 8
1 SERVING 228 KCAL/0.7G FAT
PREPARATION TIME 20 MINUTES
COOKING TIME 5 MINUTES

1 × 220g sponge flan case
4 large limes
1 × 405g can light condensed milk, chilled overnight
6 sheets leaf gelatine
1 vanilla pod
200g (7oz) virtually fat free fromage frais
300g (11oz) Quark (low-fat soft cheese)
2 egg whites
fresh berries to decorate
icing sugar to dust

1 Lightly grease an adjustable flan ring; then press it into the sponge case, just inside the outside edge. Remove the outside edge and discard. Line the ring with parchment paper.
2 Finely grate the lime zest from all 4 limes into a mixing bowl and add the condensed milk.
3 Using an electric mixer, whisk on high speed until thick and double in volume.
4 Soak the gelatine in cold water, then drain, squeezing out any excess water from the gelatine.
5 Cut the limes in half and squeeze out the juice into a small saucepan. Split the vanilla pod lengthways, using a sharp knife, and scrape out the black seeds from the centre.

6 Add the vanilla seeds and the gelatine to the pan. Heat
   gently, stirring continuously, until the gelatine has
   dissolved.
7 Whisk the hot syrup into the milk until fully combined.
   Carefully fold in the fromage frais and Quark until smooth.
8 Whisk the egg whites until stiff peaks. Fold into the
   mixture, using a large metal spoon, and then pour into the
   ring.
9 Refrigerate for 4 hours, ideally overnight, until set.
10 Decorate with fresh berries and dust with icing sugar before
   serving.

Baked stuffed apple Ⓥ

SERVES 1
1 SERVING 100 KCAL/0.3G FAT
PREPARATION TIME 5 MINUTES
COOKING TIME 30 MINUTES

1 large cooking apple
25g (1oz) dried fruit
1 tsp honey

1 Preheat the oven to 200C, 400F, Gas Mark 6.
2 Remove the core from the apple but leave the apple intact.
   Score with a sharp knife around the 'waist' of the apple,
   cutting through only the skin.
3 Mix together the dried fruit and the honey and pile into the
   centre of the apple. Place in an ovenproof dish and bake in
   the oven for about 30 minutes.

Baked banana ⓥ

SERVES 1
PER SERVING 103 KCAL/0.2G FAT
PREPARATION TIME 5 MINUTES
COOKING TIME 30 MINUTES

1 banana
pinch of brown sugar
1 tbsp raisins
pinch of cinnamon

1 Preheat the oven to 180C, 350F, Gas Mark 4.
2 Peel and slice the banana and place in a shallow ovenproof
   dish. Sprinkle the brown sugar, raisins and cinnamon on top.
3 Pour 4 tbsps of water over the banana and bake in the oven
   for 30 minutes.

Baked egg custard ⓥ

SERVES 2
1 SERVING 109 KCAL/5.6G FAT
PREPARATION TIME 15 MINUTES
COOKING TIME 1 HOUR

300ml (½ pint) skimmed milk
2 egg yolks
sugar or sweetener to taste
a little nutmeg (optional)

1 Preheat the oven to 160C, 325F, Gas Mark 2.
2 Place the milk in a pan and heat until it 'steams'.

3 Lightly beat the egg yolks in a bowl until smooth.
4 Pour the hot milk onto the eggs and mix well. Sweeten to taste with sugar or sweetener. Strain into a small pie dish and sprinkle a little nutmeg over (if using).
5 Half-fill a small roasting tin with water. Place the pie dish in the roasting tin and place in the oven. Bake for about 1 hour until the custard is set and firm to touch.

14 Get active

If you think that exercise is not for you, think again. The benefits you will reap from even a modest amount will far outweigh the effort you have to put in. This chapter will help you identify a starting point for exercise and then guide you realistically through a programme which will enable you to increase your fitness gradually.

As I explained earlier, aerobic exercise helps you to burn fat. Any exercise that makes you breathe more deeply works your heart and lungs harder than normal. This type of exercise is called aerobic because it means 'with oxygen'. Oxygen is simply a fuel, like the petrol in your car. But just as we can't put crude oil into our petrol tanks – it has to be refined – the oxygen needs additional components to be converted into the energy we need to exercise, and this conversion takes place in our muscles.

When we perform aerobic-type activities such as walking or jogging, we are forced to breathe more deeply as our lungs demand extra oxygen. The heart beats faster and pumps more blood around the body, carrying the oxygen to where it is needed, all around the body. The good news is that the oxygen is also getting to the surface of the skin as well as to the muscles.

This is important when we are trying to lose weight and want to encourage the skin to shrink back. But it gets even better.

When we start exercising aerobically, it is as if the body switches on its central heating and starts burning extra fuel. The fuel is manufactured in the muscles, but to make this fuel, three components are needed. The first component is the extra oxygen we are breathing in and which is being carried around the body in the blood. The second is an engine to fire up the burning of the fuel, and in our muscles we have lots of tiny engines called mitochondria. The third component is real fuel to burn, and this comes from our fat stores around and inside our muscles. When exercising aerobically try to visualise your body fat being burned in the oxygen flame!

Once our bodies are warm, we can keep going for a very long time because we are literally making the fuel needed to continue from the extra oxygen we are breathing in. Interestingly, we burn more fat if we exercise at a moderate and steady level – such as going for a long walk or doing a moderate level of aerobics for 30–40 minutes – than going for a sprint, because extremely energetic activities don't use the same fat-burning fuel system. The good news is that as soon as you become a regular exerciser you stimulate your fat cells to release their fat stores more easily.

The more regularly we work out aerobically, the more mito-chondria (little engines) we create in our muscles, which helps our muscles burn fat even more effectively. And that means that we will find it easier to stay lean and trim in the long term.

So whenever we do aerobic exercise we will definitely be burning body fat as well as strengthening our heart and lungs. The two go hand in hand. When we understand the physiology behind aerobic exercise it is easy to understand why endurance athletes are so lean.

The key to maximising our weight loss, or to be brutal, our fat loss, is to find a form of exercise we enjoy, otherwise we just won't do it. Despite being in the fitness business for more than 30 years, there are only a few types of exercise that I enjoy. I hate swimming, loathe running or going on an exercise bike and have recently given away all the gym equipment that I have had for 10 years or so and hardly ever used at home!

The forms of exercise I do enjoy are walking, and exercising to music, such as aerobics or salsacise, and that's why I continue to teach my diet and fitness classes. But my greatest number of active calories are probably spent throughout the week by generally being active. I dash about, do my errands, run up and down stairs and cram a huge amount into my very busy life. But just being active on its own would not be enough to keep me in good shape, because I would not be working out at a level that elevates my heart rate to call on my fat stores and keep me slim and fit. To do that we have to breathe more deeply for 20–30 minutes at a time – the sort of workout that you get at my classes or by exercising to one of my videos or DVDs.

Unless you introduce some form of activity into your lifestyle you will find that your weight-loss progress is slow and your figure will not be in as good shape as it could be. Despite my advancing years, I have a better figure now than I did in my twenties and that has only been achieved by eating a low-fat diet and doing some proper aerobic exercise every week over a very long time. It does not mean you have to join an expensive gym or start training to run the London Marathon. Just go to a fitness class on a regular basis. I have run exercise classes in Leicester every Monday evening for as long as I can remember. Around 15 of my members have been attending for well over 20 years and they have good figures and are basically fit. Even though that class is the only formal exercise that most of them do each week, it has made a difference to their fitness levels and their figures. So don't ever think 'anything' isn't enough. Doing 'something' makes an enormous difference, particularly if it is over a long period of time.

In this book I have included a progressive walking programme that will help you become fitter and slimmer. For those of you who would like to give jogging a try, I have also included a progressive jogging programme. The key is to start slowly and allow your body to develop its fitness over a period of time. And just in case you are thinking you couldn't possibly start running at your age, I recently met a delightful lady called Renée Clarke. She took up running at the age of 58 because she didn't want to get bored when she retired. She is now 79 years young and, when I met her, she had just completed her 14th London Marathon and, in all, has completed a total of 40 marathons around the world! Perhaps we should all stop making excuses!

The experts tell us that, ideally, we should aim to do some aerobic activity five times a week for 20–30 minutes. It sounds daunting, but realise that as well as your regular (hopefully) aerobics session you may be doing housework, gardening, playing with the children, walking the dog. They all count. We also need to include some regular strength work or 'body toning' to help us achieve and keep a good body shape and to increase our muscle mass, which helps us to maintain our metabolic rate.

As well as designing the walking and jogging programmes in this book, my good friend Mary Morrris, who is Head of Training and Development at Rosemary Conley Diet and Fitness Clubs, has helped me create for you a time-efficient toning programme that contains the best and most effective body toning exercises. Do the exercises regularly, and you will transform your shape while investing only a few minutes of your time each week.

Also, my latest Shape Up & Salsacise DVD is designed to give you a fun salsacise, aerobic fat-burning workout plus a body conditioning session that incorporates a resistance band to maximise the benefits to your muscle tone. By using a resistance band you will be able to challenge your muscles further, which makes the workout even more effective.

The key to any form of activity is to do it regularly. You wouldn't expect to improve your game of tennis or golf if you played just twice a year. Similarly, If you want to improve your body shape you need to practise the exercises regularly. Over a period of weeks, and months, you will see an enormous difference, which will enable you to wear – and look fabulous in – stylish clothes.

HOW MANY CALORIES DO YOU BURN?

Activity	approx. no. of calories burned in 30 minutes
Aerobic dance	300
Walking	200
Running	300
Stair climbing	245
Swimming	280
Cycling	245
Rowing	240
Tennis (singles)	230
(doubles)	85
Skating	260

Walking

Walking is a form of aerobic exercise that everyone can incorporate into their daily routine without too much effort. With every passing decade, we have needed to walk less and less each day, due in part to our sedentary lifestyles and our reliance on the car. However, if you change the way you think about walking, particularly because you now know it helps you to burn fat and keeps you healthy, you can find lots of opportunities in the working day to increase the amount of walking you do.

For instance, avoid using the lift when the stairs are right next to it, park the car further away from the entrance to the office. Try walking to school with your children if it's fine weather and do them a favour, too. You could even have two days a week when you leave the car at home and find ways of getting to work that involve walking for part of the journey, for instance by getting off the bus a couple of stops earlier. No need to put on any kit or set a special time aside, it is the 'anywhere, any time' type of exercise that can make a major contribution to your fitness and fat burning. For a progressive walking programme, see page 257.

Swimming

Swimming can also make a major contribution to your heart and lung efficiency. It uses muscles throughout the whole body and is truly aerobic, which ensures a high level of fat-burning. Gradually decrease the frequency with which you stop to get your breath back and aim to swim continuously at a steady pace for 20 minutes.

Cycling

If you used to enjoy cycling when you were young, the chances are you would easily enjoy it as an adult. Make the commitment of buying a bike and get out on the open road to improve your aerobic fitness. The advantages of cycling over walking and jogging is that you can cover greater distances in a relatively short space of time. If you can get out into the countryside, you have the added benefits of fresh air and scenery. One word of advice: if you do take up cycling treat yourself to some padded cycling shorts as these make cycling long distances much more comfortable. Take a water bottle to sip from too. Dehydration is one of the key factors in causing fatigue, so keep hydrated during cycling or indeed any form of aerobic exercise.

The development of the National Cycle Network in the UK means that you will be able to cycle safely away from traffic, pollution and noise. For more information visit www.sustrans.org.uk or contact the Sustrans information line on 0845 113 0065.

Another option is to do a charity bike ride. It gives you a goal, encourages you to train and does a load of good for charity too. If you decide to do a charity bike ride, build up your distances gradually and keep a record of the miles you achieve. After each ride do the stretches on pages 264–5. These are very important as they will help you avoid discomfort later.

Jogging

Jogging is one of the most effective ways of developing excellent heart and lung fitness and controlling weight. The pressure on the joints can be a problem and you should build up through a walking phase first to reduce the risk of injury. If you have a bad back or are very overweight at the start of the programme, proceed with caution.

Most people who start a jogging programme try to do too much too soon making it impossible to sustain. The progressive jogging programme on page 261 is different because it shows you how to build up gradually. If you are determined to stick with it you will succeed. To help you stay motivated, buy a pedometer and use it consistently over the period of time that you build up your jogging.

The programme in this book recommends that you start with a walking phase. Continuous walking will slowly prepare your legs for the next jogging phase and will also help you to develop a consistent routine. The programme always takes exactly 30 minutes and you are advised to do it three times a week. It builds from exclusively walking to jogging over a period of 12 weeks. Once you can run for 30 minutes three times a week you will be doing a massive amount to help your lung fitness. Combine this with some aerobics or salsacise sessions and you'll be well on your way. To tone your muscles simply add the Gi Jeans toning programme on the other days of the week.

Find the right workout for YOU

If you want to be more physically active but don't know where to start because exercise isn't something you have been doing regularly or you can't find an exercise you enjoy enough to stick with, try the following quiz. It will show you which type of workout will suit you the best.

How the quiz works

There are four key areas that motivate us to exercise – appearance (how we look), social (whether we enjoy exercising in company or alone), fitness (desire for a strong, fit, healthy body) and interest and enjoyment (whether exercising is a joy or a chore). The statements below relate to one of those four areas. Now read each item and decide on a scale of 1–7 how true it is for you with regard to an activity that you already do or one that you would consider doing, with 7 being 'very true' and 1 being 'not at all true to me'. Enter your score in the boxes provided.

Find the exercise that suits your personality

A1 I want to lose weight to look better ☐
E1 I want exercise to be fun ☐
F1 I want to be physically fit ☐
S1 I want to exercise with my friends ☐
A2 I want to change my shape ☐
E2 I like to do certain specific activities ☐
F2 I want to have more energy ☐
S2 I like to be with others who also like exercise and activity ☐
A3 I want to improve my appearance ☐
E3 Exercise makes me happy ☐
F3 I like activities that are physically demanding ☐
S3 I want to meet new people ☐
A4 I want to be attractive to others ☐
E4 Exercise interests me enough to keep doing it ☐

continued...

F4 I want my heart and lungs to work better ☐

S4 My friends and family want me to exercise ☐

A5 I will feel physically unattractive if I don't exercise ☐

E5 I really enjoy certain activities ☐

F5 I want to stay strong and supple ☐

S5 I enjoy spending time with others doing certain
    activities ☐

A6 I like to know I am burning lots of calories and
    getting slimmer ☐

E6 I find certain activities stimulating ☐

F6 I want to maintain my physical health and
    wellbeing ☐

S6 I work out harder in the company of other
    exercisers ☐

A7 I want to drop a dress size so I can wear
    nicer clothes ☐

E7 I like the buzz after doing the activity ☐

F7 I want to be more toned ☐

S7 I don't like being physically active on my own ☐

Now add up your scores for each category to find
your final score:

Appearance
A1 + A2 + A3 + A4 + A5 + A6 + A7 = ☐

Enjoyment/Interest
E1 + E2 + E3 + E4 + E5 + E6 + E7 = ☐

Fitness
F1 + F2 + F3 + F4 + F5 + F6 + F7 = ☐

Social

S1 + S2 + S3 + S4 + S5 + S6 + S7 =   ☐

Final score of 36–49

You are highly motivated in this category

Final score of 22–35

You are moderately motivated.

Final score of 7–21

A low area of motivation

What the scores show

By finding out where your motivation lies, you can find the fitness routine best suited to your personality. If you score highly in more than one section that just means you have even more reasons to keep active.

Appearance motivator

A high score means you are highly motivated by how you look. This means you no doubt like your body to look its best, so conditioning exercises that tone and shape your body are ideal for you. Try using a toning/resistance band or weights for faster results.

If losing weight is also important to you, choose fat-burning aerobic exercises. My Ultimate Whole Body Workout and my Shape Up & Salsacise video/DVDs feature the perfect mix of aerobic and body toning for shaping up. Work out at least three times a week to guarantee results.

Fitness motivator

A high score here is fantastic, as it means you are concerned for your overall health. Chances are, you will already be doing some sort of regular exercise, but if you'd like to move your regime up a gear, why not try increasing your exercise routine by a few minutes or fitting in an extra class or gym visit?

For the ultimate in advice and attention, you could even employ a personal trainer. If you want to get fit but don't know where to start, never underestimate the benefits of a brisk walk/gentle jog. Use a pedometer to track your progress and to encourage you to increase your walking levels.

Social motivator

If you have a high score it means you need to do activities in the company of others to increase your motivation. This is where my Diet and Fitness classes come into their own because you can not only benefit from the weekly weigh in and dietary advice, you can work out safely and effectively under the guidance of a professionally qualified instructor who is trained to advise you individually.

You probably need an exercise 'buddy' so that you can go walking together. Progress to doing a 30-minute walk five times a week or, if you can manage an hour, three times a week. Or you could attend group fitness sessions, or dance classes. Another idea is to join a club, for example running, badminton or tennis, where you will meet other people who share your interests. I recommend three fitness sessions a week to start with.

Interest/enjoyment motivator

This is a key factor in sustaining motivation. If you are forcing yourself to do an activity that you don't enjoy, it probably won't last long. If you scored high here, then you are on the right route to either keeping up your exercise programme or embarking on one that you will enjoy.

But don't worry if you had a low score. If gyms and the like put you off exercise, consider slightly less conventional but beneficial forms such as golf, horse-riding, squash, badminton, cycling, trampolining, dancing and salsacise.

Fitting exercise into your life

Starting an exercise programme from scratch, and sticking to it, means making some changes to how you spend your leisure time. It depends how much you want to be in better shape and how realistic you are about how long it will take. Look at times in the week when it would be possible to be more active. The jogging programme on pages 261–3 takes only 30 minutes of your time, but you do need to select a time when you can be sure you will stick to it. Finding an exercise 'buddy' will considerably increase your chances of doing so because few of us like to let people down and once an arrangement is made you are likely to follow it through.

Look at the sample exercise planner overleaf to see how you can achieve a balanced programme. Now, plan your own weekly exercise schedule, using the blank version on page 309. Tick the five occasions when you are going to set aside 30 minutes for your aerobic session. The toning programme can be shorter if you wish – it takes between 10 and 15 minutes to cover all the major muscle groups. Try to do this on at least two occasions a week.

SAMPLE EXERCISE PLANNER

	M	T	W	T	F	S	S
MORNING SESSION							
Aerobic workout 30 minutes	✔	☐	✔	☐	☐	☐	☐
Toning programme 10 minutes	☐	✔	☐	☐	☐	☐	☐
LUNCHTIME SESSION							
Aerobic workout 30 minutes	☐	☐	☐	☐	☐	☐	☐
Toning programme 10 minutes	☐	☐	☐	✔	☐	☐	☐
AFTERNOON/ EVENING SESSION							
Aerobic workout 30 minutes	☐	☐	☐	☐	✔	✔	✔
Toning programme 10 minutes	☐	☐	☐	✔	☐	☐	☐

15 The Gi Jeans Diet walking and jogging programmes

If you have quite a lot of weight to lose or are unfit, it's important to start with the walking programme first before you attempt the jogging programme. So start slowly and build up your fitness gradually over a period of weeks.

The walking programme

For years we have overlooked the obvious in our quest for the perfect fat-burning activity. All this time the answer has been right at our feet – good old straightforward walking! No high-impact pounding on the joints, no getting so out of breath that you can't speak, no fancy equipment or expensive clothing, and everyone can do it. The big plus is that if you begin to treat it as your workout and stick at it, you will lose fat from your body at an amazing rate! Walking is also the best activity to give you trimmer thighs. So start putting your best foot forward and follow this programme regularly.

THE BENEFITS OF WALKING

- It reduces blood pressure. Walking makes your heart and circulatory system work harder, which reduces the risk of high blood pressure.
- It reduces the risk of heart disease. Walking lowers the level of 'bad' cholesterol in the blood which is linked to heart disease.
- It tones up your muscles and strengthens your bones. Regular brisk walkers reduce their risk of suffering from osteoporosis – the thinning of the bones experienced by many women after menopause.

FIT MORE WALKING INTO EVERYDAY LIFE

- Get off the bus earlier, or park the car further away from the office.
- Park in the furthest corner of the supermarket car park!
- Use the stairs instead of the lift or escalator.
- Save the expense of driving to the shops – walk instead.
- Walking is an excellent activity for all the family, so involve them too.

How to use this programme

Whatever your fitness level or previous walking experience, this programme will suit you. Start with the Level 1 walking technique, only moving on to Level 2 when you feel ready. Always perform the stretches on pages 264–5 at the end of your walking session.

WALKING SHOES

Your body will only reach its full walking potential if you invest in a suitable pair of shoes. Walkers strike the ground hardest on the heel, so choose shoes with good heel cushioning and stability. Also the front foot flexes at almost twice the angle of a runner, so you need a shoe with good flexibility. Your local sports shop should be able to advise you on what to buy.

WALKING POSTURE
No matter how fast or how far you go, standing tall is key. Shoulders that hunch forward tighten the chest and inhibit breathing, so make sure you pull your shoulders back. Keep your chin up, always look about 10 feet ahead, and hold some tension in your tummy to support your back.

Walking technique

LEVEL 1: EASY WALK
This is a pace and style that is particularly designed for beginners and can also be referred to as your normal pace, as long as you try to keep going for the time you have set yourself. It will raise your heart rate to a low to moderate level. If you wish to stay at this level, because it is as much as you can ever manage, it will still give you all the health benefits and help you lose weight.

- Make sure your heel strikes the ground first.
- Let your arms swing naturally at your sides.
- Maintain the good posture described above.
- You will burn 100 calories in 20 minutes.

LEVEL 2: BRISK WALK
This is a much more powerful action than Level 1 and therefore uses more energy. If you can progress to a brisk walk, the fat-burning benefits will be much greater. Have a go!

- Walk with a more purposeful stride, with the heel hitting the ground squarely and the toes lifted high.
- You will then create a strong push-off from the foot behind to move you dynamically forward.
- The arms should bend from the elbows and the fingers should loosely curl, as if holding a fragile egg, rather than forming a tight fist.
- There should be a slight forward lean from the hips.
- You will burn 100 calories in 15 minutes.

Walking schedule

WEEKS 1 AND 2

Frequency: 2–3 times per week

Start off with 10–15 minutes at your normal walking pace, taking note of the techniques in Level 1. Try not to stop and admire the view!

WEEKS 3 AND 4

Frequency: 2–3 times per week

Time yourself on the outward journey, still at your normal pace, for 10 minutes. On the return journey, increase your pace slightly so that it takes less than 10 minutes.

WEEKS 5 AND 6

Frequency: 3–4 times a week

Outward journey should now be timed at 12 minutes. Try to alternate Level 1 technique with Level 2. On the first return journey, record your time and keep trying to improve on that time – even if only by a few seconds – each time you do it.

WEEKS 7 AND 8

Frequency: 4–5 times a week

Outward journeys should now be timed at 15 minutes. Prolong the periods you walk at level 2. Aim to be able to use Level 2 all the way home!

Tips for safer walking

- Always walk slowly for the first 5 minutes to warm up the muscles, including the heart.
- Gently roll your shoulders forwards and back before you really start to stride out.
- At the end of your walk, reduce to a gentler pace for around 3 minutes and then follow the stretch programme.
- Always face oncoming traffic. However, always walk on the outside of a blind bend.
- If possible walk with a friend. Otherwise tell someone where you are going and how long you will be.
- Wear light-coloured and reflective clothing, particularly at dawn or dusk.
- Petroleum jelly is a walker's best friend. Spread a little on your inner thighs, under your arms and around underwear straps to prevent chafing.
- Wear sun protection. Being outdoors more increases your risks of skin damage.

The jogging programme

If you have never walked at a brisk pace continuously for 30 minutes you may need to build up slowly. Start by trying to fit shorter bouts of walking into your normal day (even 10 minutes is a start) until you can comfortably keep going briskly for 30 minutes.

Follow the programme on just three days a week. Place a tick under columns 1, 2 and 3 as you complete each challenge. Always finish each session by doing the stretches on pages 265–6.

	DAY 1	DAY 2	DAY 3
WEEK 1 Walk 30 minutes	☐	☐	☐
WEEK 2 Walk 30 minutes Every 4th minute jog 1 minute	☐	☐	☐
WEEK 3 Jog 2 minutes, walk 4 minutes Complete sequence 5 times	☐	☐	☐
WEEK 4 Jog 3 minutes, walk 3 minutes Complete the sequence 5 times	☐	☐	☐
WEEK 5 Jog 5 minutes, walk 2½ minutes Complete sequence 4 times	☐	☐	☐
WEEK 6 Jog 7 minutes, walk 3 minutes Complete sequence 3 times	☐	☐	☐

	DAY 1	DAY 2	DAY 3

WEEK 7
Jog 8 minutes, walk 2 minutes
Complete sequence 3 times
☐ ☐ ☐

WEEK 8
Jog 9 minutes, walk 2 minutes
Complete sequence twice and
then run for 8 minutes
☐ ☐ ☐

WEEK 9
Jog 9 minutes, walk 1 minute
Complete the sequence 3 times
☐ ☐ ☐

WEEK 10
Jog 13 minutes, walk 2 minutes
Complete the sequence twice
☐ ☐ ☐

WEEK 11
Jog 14 minutes, walk 1 minute
Complete the sequence twice
☐ ☐ ☐

WEEK 12
Jog 30 minutes
☐ ☐ ☐

Stretches

Always perform these stretches after doing the walking or jogging programme.

1 Calf stretch

Standing tall, take one foot back, with the heel securely on the floor. Now bend your front knee, keeping the toes of both feet facing forwards. Take the back foot far enough away to feel a stretch in the calf of the back leg. Hold for 10 seconds, then change legs and repeat.

2 Lower calf and chest stretch

Now bring the back foot in half a step and bend both knees to feel a stretch further down the calf. Then take both hands into the small of your back and squeeze your shoulder blades together to feel a stretch across your chest. Hold for 10 seconds, then change legs and stretch the other calf.

3 Front thigh stretch

Use a wall for support if you need to. Lift your left foot off the floor and hold it near the ankle with your left hand. Make sure your standing leg is slightly bent and your knees are together. Stand tall and push your left hip slightly forwards to feel a strong stretch down the front of your left thigh. Hold for 10 seconds, then change legs and repeat.

4 Back of thigh stretch

Place your right leg straight out in front and bend your left leg. Keeping your front leg straight, place your hands on your thighs and lean forwards slightly, with your back flat, to feel a stretch down the back of your right thigh. Hold for 10 seconds, then change legs and repeat.

16 The Gi Jeans Diet toning programme

This easy-to-follow workout will tone you up from top to toe and it takes just ten minutes. Do it regularly and you will see a definite improvement in your body shape – tighter arms, shapelier bust, flatter tum, trimmer waist, firmer buttocks and thighs and a stronger back. Before you start, read the guidelines on good posture. These will help you avoid some common physical problems as well as make you look slimmer!

Posture is key

Good posture is the key to allowing all your joints to move freely. Your skeleton forms the framework of your body. If you hold your skeleton properly, then all the muscles that attach to it are allowed to move in the correct way. Poor posture can cause very serious physical problems both in the neck area and the lower back and result in long-term damage that can limit your ability to lead a full and active life. The good news is that it is possible to make real changes to the way you hold yourself that will not only help relieve any current problems but most certainly prevent new ones developing.

Neck and shoulder relaxers

If you suffer a recurring neck problem it may be partly due to the way you hold yourself, and this has probably developed over a number of years. It is not unusual to be diagnosed with a trapped nerve in the neck, which causes pain and discomfort through the shoulders and down the arms. Modern lifestyles can lead to considerable stress, making you hold your shoulders very tight. Here are a few tips on relieving tension:

- When you are feeling tense simply drop your shoulders down and relax them. At the same time try to lengthen the back of your neck as if being pulled by a string from the top of your head towards the ceiling.
- Slow your breathing down, particularly the 'out' breath and you will certainly feel calmer.
- Every hour, slowly roll your shoulders, particularly when you are working at a desk.

Avoiding lower back problems

Back problems are very common in modern life. The main problem is when we bend forwards, as the spinal muscles then have to take the strain of all our weight. These thin strips of muscle are not designed to be repeatedly put under that kind of pressure.

If you bend forwards while holding a lot of weight, for example when putting something heavy in the back of a car, not only are your back muscles strained but the connective tissue, particularly the ligaments and tendons (designed to hold the spine together) try to take some of the strain. This can cause more serious long-term damage.

Here are a few tips to help prevent back problems occurring in the first place and to help reduce the chance of a recurring back problem:

- Work on developing a good posture (see opposite). A spine held in good alignment has less work to do.
- Strengthen your natural corset – the trunk area of the body – so that the spinal column is supported by strong muscles (see exercises 1, 2 and 7 in the toning workout that follows).
- Avoid heavy lifting, particularly if you have had a back problem in the past.
- Try not to carry shoulder bags on just one shoulder as this affects alignment. Instead, carry the bag on your back, or diagonally across your front, so that the weight is evenly distributed.
- Always bend your knees to pick anything up from the floor and keep your back as straight as possible.
- If you have young children, avoid holding them on one hip for long periods as this puts too much pressure on one side and can push the pelvis out of line.
- Keep as active as possible. If sitting for long periods, try to get up and move about every hour or so.
- Attend exercise classes that include back exercises. All RCD&F classes will advise you how to care for your back and give you the right exercises to do.

Quick posture check

- Stand with feet hip distance apart and parallel.
- Soften your knees so they are not locked out, as this puts a strain on the knee joints.
- Gently pull your tummy in a little. Unless you are doing specific exercises, don't aim to hold it in too tightly during the day as it is impossible to do that for too long.
- Concentrate on drawing your shoulders back and at the same time relax them down.
- Lengthen the back of your neck, keeping your chin parallel to the floor. It should feel as if you are being pulled up from the top of your head towards the ceiling. This has the beneficial effect of separating the vertebrae in the neck.

The ten-minute tone-up

Practise this programme regularly – at least three times a week – and you will see a definite improvement in your body shape.

Top tips for success

- Always hold your tummy in tight to support your back in every exercise you do.
- Breathe evenly throughout each exercise – breathe out on the 'exertion' and in as you release.

- Do every exercise slowly so that you concentrate on your technique and have time to do each exercise really well.
- When you have completed your repetitions, do the stretches given for each toning exercise. These will not only help your muscles to recover but also contribute to your overall flexibility and the range of movement in your joints.

1 THE BEST EXERCISE FOR A FLAT TUMMY

Gone are the days of hundreds of sit-ups to give you a flat tummy! We now know that one of the best exercises is simply to pull your tummy in as tight as you can for about 10 seconds several times a day. There is still a huge value, though, in adding some slow and controlled curl-ups with the tummy held in tight as this makes all the abdominal muscles work together.

Tummy toner

- Lie on your back with knees bent and feet flat on the floor, hip distance apart. Place both hands well behind your head without clasping them.

- Now draw your tummy button in very tight as if trying to attach it to your spine but without losing the natural curve in your spine, and hold it there. Breathe in and, as you begin to breathe out, lift your head and shoulders slightly off the

floor, supporting the weight of your head in your hands. Slowly release but keep your tummy held tight.

- Do 4 repetitions, then rest. Continue doing sets of 4 until you feel you have done enough.
- To work harder, try to lift higher and hold at the top for 2 seconds before lowering to the floor.

Abdominal stretch

- Turn on to your front and place your hands close to your shoulders, with elbows in line with your shoulders.

- Lift your upper body and support yourself on your elbows, keeping your shoulders relaxed and your neck long. Now gently lift your chin slightly to feel a stretch right down the front of your trunk. Hold for 10 seconds, then release.

2 THE BEST EXERCISE FOR A TRIM WAIST

There are two sets of waist muscles, called the obliques, and they form the perfect corset for the trunk. Doing exercises specifically for the waist adds real shape to the trunk while at the same time supporting your back, so exercising this area is a real must if you have had back problems. To work these muscles effectively you need to twist (or bend) the waist area, pulling those muscles in the best direction to tighten them – just like drawing the laces on a corset!

Waist trimmer

- Lie on your back with legs in the air directly above your hips, knees slightly bent and hands behind your head. Your elbows should be only just in view and the back of your neck should be long and relaxed.
- Now pull your tummy in very tight before slowly lifting your head and shoulders just off the floor and reach your right hand towards your left foot so that your trunk twists slightly. Release back down before lifting your left hand towards your right foot. Keep changing sides for 8 repetitions, or less if you need to. Breathe out as you lift and in as you lower.

- As an easier alternative you can leave your feet on the floor, with knees bent, and simply reach each hand in turn towards the outside of each knee. Repeat in sets of 8 repetitions until you feel you have done enough.

Waist stretch

- Sit upright with legs in a comfortable position (sit on a chair if you prefer). Now reach up your left hand towards the ceiling, with your other hand on the floor or chair seat to support your trunk.
- Now lift your raised hand higher and then bend to the right towards the supporting hand. Try not to lean forwards or back and keep reaching as if trying to touch the ceiling. Both hips must stay well down. Hold for 10 seconds, then change sides and repeat.

3 THE BEST EXERCISE FOR SMOOTH OUTER THIGHS

The muscles that lie on the outside of the hips are extremely important in keeping the hips stable to support the hip joints and aid balance. Doing specific exercises to target that area on a regular basis keeps the hips and thighs firm and in good shape. Walking is an excellent way to tone the thighs, particularly the front of the thighs (quadriceps), but the outer and inner thighs do not get the same level of work, so it is good to spend time on them in your toning programme.

Outer thigh lift

- Lie on your right side with your right arm extended along the floor and a towel on top of the arm to support your head and ensure the neck is in a good alignment. Bring both legs to a 90-degree angle and then straighten the top leg, while pressing the sole of the foot away to create tension down the whole leg (a). Make sure the hips are stacked on top of each other and that you can just see the toes of the extended leg.

a

b

- Now lift the leg slowly and under control as far as you can without tipping the hip backwards (b). Slowly lower again. Keep lifting and lowering, maintaining the push away with the sole of the foot and with tummy held in tight to keep you stable.

- Start with 12 repetitions on one leg and then roll over and repeat on the other leg. Aim to gradually increase the number of repetitions over time.

Outer thigh stretch

- Sit upright with both legs stretched out in front and with your spine relaxed. Bring your left leg over your right knee and place that foot on the floor beside your right knee. Place your left hand on the floor slightly behind your left hip and place your right hand on the outside of the left knee.

- Now sit up straight, with shoulders down and neck long. Using your right hand to draw your left knee further across your trunk to feel a stretch in the left hip. Hold for 10 seconds, then change sides and repeat.

4 THE BEST EXERCISE FOR FIRM INNER THIGHS

We would have to walk sideways like a crab if we were to keep the inner thigh muscles (adductors) working hard all day! This is one reason why the inner thighs can become very flabby, and if you are very overweight they can even rub together and cause considerable discomfort. To firm them up effectively you need to do specific exercises to make them work independently of the other leg muscles and get them to tighten up. Adding ankle weights can really speed up the toning process.

Inner thigh lift

- Lie on your side with your head propped up comfortably on your elbow. Bend the top leg over the bottom leg and rest the top knee on a towel to align the hips. Fully straighten the bottom leg, pulling the toes towards your body and pushing the heel away.

- Lift and lower the bottom leg under control. Try keeping the leg just off the floor as you lower so that you work harder. Repeat 12 times, then rest and either repeat another set or change sides and repeat.

Inner thigh stretch

There are only a few stretches that play a key role in helping us to become more flexible and this is one of them. Maintaining a good range of movement in the hips is important if you are to avoid hip problems in older age.

- Sit upright with soles of the feet together and hands around your ankles. Try to position your elbows just inside your knees.
- Now, using pressure from your elbows, gently press your knees further towards the floor and hold for 10 seconds. Continue to hold the stretch as you breathe in and, as you breathe out, press the knees down further for another 10 seconds.

5 THE BEST EXERCISE FOR A LIFTED BOTTOM

The buttocks area is one that really does benefit hugely from regular exercise. Simply going up and down stairs is one of the best exercises for lifting and firming the bottom, but if you add on this very effective exercise as well, you will see a big difference in no time. Using ankle weights will firm up this area more quickly.

Rear leg raise

- Position yourself on your forearms and knees, with elbows directly under your shoulders and knees under your hips. Pull your tummy in tight to support your back, and keep your head in line with your spine to prevent tension in the neck. Place your left knee further back slightly, with the foot off the floor (a).

a

b

- Pull the toes of your back foot down to flex the foot and then lift the leg up and press the sole of the foot towards the ceiling (b). Lower again under control. Repeat 12 times, then change legs and repeat. Build up your repetitions gradually, aiming to doing another set on each leg.

Back of thigh and hip stretch

● Lie on your back with both knees bent. Take hold behind one knee and draw it in towards your chest.

● Now extend that leg towards the ceiling and try to straighten it as much as possible. Make sure both hips stay firmly fixed to the floor and keep the neck and shoulders relaxed. Hold for 10 seconds, then take a deep breath in and, as you breathe out, try to straighten the leg further or, if already very straight, bring the thigh closer to your chest. Hold for a further 10 seconds. You should feel a strong stretch in the back of the thigh. Repeat with the other leg.

6 THE BEST EXERCISE FOR A SHAPELY BUST AND TIGHT UNDERARMS

This is often an area of considerable weakness in women as they tend to focus on exercises for the tummy area, and the hips and thighs. This is not a good idea, as you will be neglecting some key muscle groups that help to give your bust a lift and prevent flabby underarms. The press-up is a wonderful exercise for this area. It can be made easy or hard, so it suits many different levels of ability and gives fantastic results in both the chest area and the underarms.

Press-up

● Start on your hands and knees in a square box shape, with hands under your shoulders, knees under your hips, and tummy pulled in very tight to support your back. Depending on your ability, you can either stay in that position or try taking the knees further back as shown (a). The latter makes the exercise harder as you now have to push more body weight up.

a

b

- Breathe in as you slowly lower your forehead down in front of your hands, pushing your elbows outwards and keeping your tummy held in tight (b). Now breathe out as you lift without fully straightening your elbows. Repeat 8 times, then rest and repeat another set of 8.

Chest stretch
This stretch is one of the most important for the upper body as it helps compensate for sitting in a rounded position in a chair all day and can really help to improve posture.

- Sitting upright, place both hands just behind your hips on the floor and draw your shoulders back to feel a stretch in the chest area. Hold for 10 seconds, then release.

Underarm stretch

- Still sitting upright, take your right hand behind your right shoulder. Keep your head up and your back straight.
- Using your left hand on the back of the right arm, gently push the right hand further down your back to feel a stretch in the underarm. Hold for 10 seconds, then change arms and repeat.

7 THE BEST EXERCISE FOR A STRONG AND TROUBLE-FREE BACK

Practise this exercise and the tummy and waist exercises (1 and 2) regularly and you will be doing a lot to help keep your spine in good condition. We bend forwards a lot throughout the day and this puts a lot of strain on the back. The spinal extension exercise opposite makes the spine work hard in the opposite direction to help strengthen the back muscles, while the shoulder lift is excellent for the posture muscles, located at the back of the shoulders.

Back exercises are best done daily, particularly if you have had trouble in the past. If you currently have a back condition you may have been advised not to do this exercise by a physio-therapist or other medical professional.

Spinal extension with shoulder lift

- Lie on your front with your arms by your sides and your forehead in contact with the floor (a). (If you have a back problem, place your arms out in front of you and keep them on the floor.)

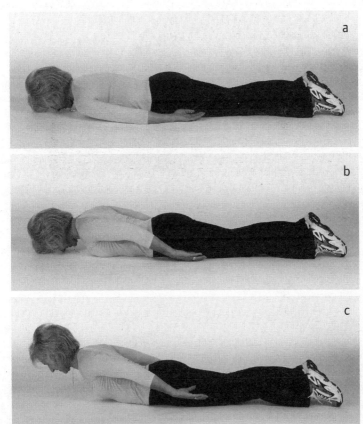

- Now draw your shoulders back and down (b) before lifting your forehead off the floor just a few inches (c). Hold for 2 seconds, then slowly release. Repeat 6 times only, then rest. Repeat another set if you can.

Spinal stretch

- Position yourself on hands and knees, with hands under your shoulders and knees under your hips.

- Now pull your tummy in tight and arch the centre of the spine up towards the ceiling, pulling your head down between your shoulders and drawing your hips closer to the centre of your body. Hold for 10 seconds, then release.

17 Maintaining your new weight

Losing weight is relatively straightforward but keeping it off is an even greater challenge! I have to admit, I get frustrated when I read negative press relating to 'diets failing' when people regain their lost weight. It gives the impression that you might as well not bother to try 'because it will all go back anyway'.

Overweight is not a curable disease but it is a manageable one and, providing your method of dieting incorporates lifestyle changes and is not a quick-fix, there is absolutely no reason why you shouldn't maintain your new weight in the long term.

When I first wrote my Hip and Thigh Diet in 1988 I ran a trial with around 100 dieters following the diet plan for eight weeks. The book went on to become an international bestseller. In the early 90s the sceptics were still very vocal about weight maintenance, so I contacted my trial team to see how they were faring five years on. Out of the 100 dieters in the trial team, 71 per cent had kept within 25 per cent of their original weight loss when the trial was run. Many had gone on to lose more weight and were very happy with their new bodies. Some of them still send me Christmas cards to tell me they are still at their goal weight! The most common comment that emerged from the team was that low-fat eating was now a way of life: 'It's not a "diet", it's just a way of eating'.

If you have followed the Gi Jeans Diet programme, you should now be well into the swing of low-fat, low-Gi eating and increased activity, and the good habits that you have acquired during your health and fitness campaign will stand you in good stead for life. So, once you have reached your desired weight, don't go back to your old bad habits. If you do go back to the eating habits that made you overweight in the first place, and to being totally inactive, you WILL regain your excess weight. This diet won't fail. It is the decision to stick with and not stray from your new healthy eating and exercise habits that will determine your long-term success. Eating healthily and keeping active will pay enormous dividends, not just in terms of your weight and your body shape but also in terms of your overall health and well-being. You've done the tough bit; now hold on to that progress.

However, you can now relax the rules a little and increase the quantities of food you eat. You may add a few more dressings to salads and eat a little low-fat hard cheese, but if you are to maintain your new figure and energy levels you will still need to follow a predominantly low-fat, low-Gi formula and take regular exercise.

The good news is that after a few weeks on a low-fat eating regime, your taste buds adapt and so it should be relatively simple to stick with your new way of eating and keep the excess weight off for good. Try to follow the eating guidelines in the Traffic Lights guide on pages 100–3. This itemises foods that form the basis of a healthy diet and that will enable you to maintain your new lower weight and foods which should only be eaten occasionally or avoided altogether if possible. You may select freely from the GREEN list without worrying about quantities unless it specifies 'in moderation'. You may also select occasionally from the AMBER list, but try to avoid items from the RED list.

Keep an eye on the scales and the fit of your waistband. If you find you are gaining weight again, return to the Gi Jeans Diet or cut back on the quantities you are eating. If you take immediate action, you can remedy any damage quite swiftly.

Ten tips for successful weight maintenance

1 Eat three meals a day and eat low-fat, low-Gi, high-volume foods. Not only will these fill you up, they will cause your body to work harder and burn more calories during the digestion process.

2 Remember that the fat you eat becomes fat on your body. If you want to stay lean you have to eat lean. Use the Traffic Light guide on the following pages for a quick and easy check on which foods to eat and which to avoid.

3 Don't eat anything other than fruit between meals. Snacking on high-fat crisps or biscuits will cause a load of damage to your waistline and will just create a habit which you will need to break if you want to stay slim. Just don't start the habit.

4 Avoid temptation by not keeping biscuits and sweets in easy reach. Instead, have plenty of fresh fruit available and keep the refrigerator stocked with low-calorie drinks and low-fat yogurts to satisfy sweet cravings.

5 Don't skip meals, since this can lead to uncontrolled eating later, and always eat breakfast to help kick-start your metabolism each day.

6 Drink alcohol in moderation only. The calories from alcohol do count and if you have too much too often you will find weight maintenance difficult. The problem with drink is that it weakens your willpower and increases your appetite so it causes a double-whammy!

7 The occasional indiscretion is not the end of the world, but do remember that one lapse can lead to another, so indulge with caution! Don't let a minor lapse become a major relapse.

8 Weigh yourself no more than once a week. Try to be relaxed about your weight and try to gauge your progress more by the fit of your clothes.

9 Continue to be as physically active as possible. If you can keep active for 30 minutes on five days a week and also do some toning exercises to keep your muscles strong and in good shape, you will almost certainly stay slim.

10 Remember that *you* are in control of your body and your lifestyle. If you want to stay slim and fit, you *can* do it.

Traffic light guide to foods

GREEN
You can consume most of these foods freely, but do restrict the quantities where specified.

- Alcohol: do not exceed 21 units a week for women and 28 units a week for men
- Beans, lentils and pulses: any type
- Bread: multigrain without added fat (i.e. not fried, no butter or margarine)
- Breakfast cereals: oats, barley, wheat bran, high-fibre varieties are best. Special K is also low Gi

- Cheese: cottage cheese, fromage frais, Quark and any cheese with max. 5% fat
- Condiments: (see also Sauces) any type
- Crispbreads: rye crispbreads, Ryvita or other low-fat, high-fibre brands
- Dressings: lemon juice, oil-free dressing, vinegar, any dressing with 5% or less fat; reduced-oil dressings in moderation
- Drinks: water, all low-calorie drinks, tea, coffee, low-fat chocolate (max. 5%) or malted drinks, made with water
- Eggs: egg whites can be eaten freely. Limit whole eggs to 4 a week
- Fish (including shellfish): any type, e.g. cod, plaice, halibut, whiting, lemon sole, cockles, crab, lobster, mussels, oysters, prawns, salmon, shrimps, tuna in brine, mackerel, herrings, kippers, sardines in tomato sauce, rollmop herrings, sprats – all cooked without butter and not fried
- Flour: wholegrain
- Fruit: any type of fresh, frozen or canned fruit, except avocado, coconut and olives; dried fruit in moderation
- Fruit juices: apple juice, exotic fruit juices, grapefruit, grape juice, unsweetened orange and pineapple
- Game: any type, roasted, without fat and with all skin removed
- Grains: any type
- Gravy: made with gravy powder or low-fat granules (max. 5% fat)
- Jams, preserves and spreads: honey, jam, Marmite, Bovril, marmalade, syrup – all in moderation
- Meat: any lean red meat cooked without fat, low-fat sausages (max. 5% fat)

- Meat substitutes: Quorn, vegeburgers, soya, tofu
- Milk: skimmed or semi-skimmed
- Nuts: chestnuts only
- Offal: any type cooked without fat
- Pasta: any type served without fat
- Pickles and relishes: any type in moderation
- Pizza: any type with 5% or less fat
- Poultry: chicken, duck, turkey – all cooked without fat and with all skin removed
- Prepared meals: any brand with 5% or less fat
- Puddings: custard (made with skimmed milk), fresh fruit salad, low-fat fromage frais, fruit cooked with wine, jelly, meringues, rice pudding made with skimmed milk, low-fat yogurt, pavlova made with yogurt, any readymade pudding with 5% or less fat
- Rice: basmati or long-grain brown, boiled or steamed
- Sauces: apple, brown, cranberry, horseradish, mint, tomato ketchup, fruity, soy sauce, low-fat white sauces, Worcestershire, tartare
- Snacks: any type with 5% or less fat
- Soups: any brands with 5% or less fat
- Stuffing: made with water
- Sugar: any type in moderation, artificial sweeteners
- Vegetables: any type cooked and served without fat
- Yogurt: any brand with 5% or less fat

AMBER

You may occasionally select items from this list.

- Bread: multigrain bread spread with low-fat spreads
- Cakes and biscuits: Jaffa cakes, filo pastry, oat cakes and high-fibre biscuits

- Cheese: cheese spread, Edam, Gouda, low-fat hard cheese, low-fat soft cheese
- Confectionery: any fat-free types
- Dressings: low-fat mayonnaise
- Drinks: low-fat malted drinks such as low-fat brands of Horlicks, Ovaltine, drinking chocolate - all made with skimmed milk or water; tea and coffee with skimmed or semi-skimmed milk; yogurt drinks
- Egg and egg products: all types in moderation; Yorkshire pudding made with skimmed milk and cooked in a non-stick baking tin without fat
- Fats and spreads: low-fat spreads with 10% or less fat
- Fish: fish fingers (grilled), fish in sauces (branded products)
- Jams and preserves: lemon curd in moderation
- Meat and meat products: beef burgers (grilled), corned beef, faggots, lamb chops (grilled), sausages (grilled), meat with some fat such as streaky bacon, roast meat
- Milk, cream and similar products: Sugar Free Dream Topping, full-fat milk, single cream
- Nuts and seeds: all nuts except chestnuts, sunflower seeds, pumpkin seeds
- Pizza
- Puddings: regular custard, ice-cream (except Cornish varieties), pavlova, regular rice pudding, sponge flans, trifle
- Sauces: sweet and savoury sauces made with full-fat milk (no butter), e.g. parsley sauce, white sauce
- Soups: any brand
- Take-away meals: ask for those cooked with minimal or little fat
- Vegetables: thick-cut chips, oven chips
- Yogurt: creamy yogurts, Greek yogurt

RED

These foods are not forbidden but avoid them whenever possible.

- Bread: garlic bread
- Cakes and biscuits: all cakes and pastries not included in the green and amber lists, all sweet biscuits, savoury biscuits containing cheese or butter
- Cheese: full-fat cheeses of any kind
- Confectionery: butterscotch, caramel, chocolate, fudge, toffees
- Dressings: all oils, cream dressings, French dressings, regular mayonnaise
- Drinks: cocoa and cocoa products, e.g. Ovaltine, except low-fat varieties, regular Horlicks, tea or coffee with cream
- Eggs and egg products: custard tarts, egg custards, quiches, Scotch eggs, Yorkshire pudding cooked in fat
- Fats and spreads: butter, dripping, lard, olive oil, low-fat spreads with more than 5% fat, margarine, margarines high in polyunsaturates, oil (all kinds), peanut butter, suet
- Fish: fish in batter, fried fish, fried fish cakes, fried whitebait
- Meat and meat products: black pudding, fatty meat, German sausage, haggis, Haslet, liver sausage, meat fried in breadcrumbs (e.g. fried beef burgers), meat pies, pasties, pâté (except chicken liver pâté), pork pies, salami, sausages in batter
- Milk, cream and similar products: butter, cream, double cream, Jersey milk, whipping cream
- Marzipan
- Poultry: goose, skin from any poultry
- Puddings: crème brûlée, gateaux, pastries, pies, profiteroles with chocolate sauce, roulades, soufflés

- Rice: fried rice
- Sauces: cheese sauce, Hollandaise sauce, sauces made with butter and/or cream
- Snacks: cheeselets and similar biscuits, regular crisps and similar fried snacks, peanuts
- Take-away meals: deep-fat fried foods, meals made with ghee
- Vegetables: thin or crinkle-cut chips, fried vegetables, vegetables roasted in fat

18 Tried and tested

I always find it exciting to put a new diet out to trial. Although I knew my diet would work because the calorie allowance was calculated at a level that would effect a satisfactory weight loss, the challenge was to come up with a formula that people would find satisfying and easy to follow, one that would inspire them to stick with it and see real results.

Some people may have followed umpteen diets in the past and then been disappointed when they regained some or all of their weight because they couldn't sustain that way of eating. So my Gi Jeans Diet eating plan had to be one that would encourage dieters to make long-term lifestyle changes.

When radio presenter Julie Mayer asked me to help with a new Flab Fighters slot on her new lunchtime BBC Radio Leicester show, I was just thinking about writing this book. My original Hip and Thigh Diet started with a trial on the same radio station in 1986, as well as on Radio Nottingham, so I thought, let history repeat itself!

The trial team

Julie received a bag full of post from volunteers for the diet trial and she selected five would-be slimmers from Leicestershire to come in to Radio Leicester's studios every fortnight for eight weeks. These were 51-year-old Sally Jones, a St John Ambulance volunteer from Theddingworth who also works in Sainsbury's, 32-year-old Angela Hartopp from Groby, who works as a clinic co-ordinator at a local hospital, 65-year-old retired Zena Hall from Syston, 54-year-old former police officer turned police trainer Peter Bruton from Sutton in the Elms, and 47-year-old managing director Rodney Munns from Rothley.

As well as following the diet plan, all the dieters were asked to participate in 20–30 minutes of aerobic exercise on five days a week and all were invited to attend my diet and fitness class each week.

Being part of a trial team is one thing but being weighed live on the radio is a tall order for anyone. Yet I could not have had a better team. They were all great sports over the eight-week trial period and took the whole project seriously. The other volunteers who wrote in followed the diet at home and later completed a questionnaire. And the results were astonishing.

After two weeks

The results of the radio dieters came first. After the initial two-week Gi Jeans Kick-start Diet the results were very encouraging. Sally, who had weighed in at 17st 2lb, lost 9lb; Angela, who started at 15st 5lb, lost 9½lb; Zena, who weighed 12st 12lb in week one, lost 5½lb, Peter lost 9½lb from his original 14st 11½lb, and Rodney, who had weighed in at 16st 13lb lost a remarkable 12lb in the fortnight. My dieters were thrilled to bits and I was pretty chuffed, too!

After the initial two-week Kick-start Diet the members of the trial team were given Part 2 of the Gi Jeans Diet. They were allowed an extra 300 calories each day, including a daily 100-calorie treat of any food they chose, plus two Power Snacks and an alcoholic drink each day. The only exception to this was Zena, who, at 65 years old, needed to continue with the Kick-start Diet. As the metabolic rate slows down after the age of 60, Zena had to stick to around 1200 calories a day to see a good rate of progress.

After four weeks

In week three Rodney went on a city break for a week, Angela went abroad on holiday to the sun, and Peter had a weekend away. Four weeks into the diet, Sally had lost a further 4lb (total loss 13lb), Zena an amazing 4½lb (total loss 10lb), and Angela another 4lb (total loss 13½lb) by keeping active on holiday and making careful food choices. The holiday boys, however, fared less well: Rodney lost just 1½lb (total loss 13½lb) and Peter gained 1lb, much to his disappointment.

After six weeks

After six weeks on the diet, Sally had lost another 1lb (total loss 1st), and Zena an amazing further 4lb (total loss 1st). Angela lost another 1½lb (total loss 1st 1lb), while Peter had made a massive effort to redeem himself and lost a remarkable 5lb (total loss 13½lb). Not to be outdone, Rodney had obviously put in all the effort he could and lost a further 6½lb, achieving an astonishing loss in six weeks of 1st 6lb.

I suggested that the team went back on the Gi Jeans Kick-start Diet for just one week to give them a final boost. I didn't know how this would affect their weight loss but decided it would be worth a try. They did it and achieved remarkable results.

After eight weeks

It was time for the final on-air weigh-in and they all looked SO much slimmer! Sally had lost another 4lb, taking her eight-week total loss to 1st 4lb. Zena lost a further 3½lb, making her total loss 1st 3lb. That was a truly remarkable achievement because losing weight does become more difficult as we get older. Not only that, Zena's 70-year-old husband, Michael, had been eating similar food to her and had lost 1st 7lb along the way without even trying! Angela lost a further 4½lb, taking her grand weight loss total to 1st 5lb. She looked SO different and had blossomed into a stunning, trim woman. Peter really pulled out all the stops for his final weigh-in and lost an amazing 6lb to lose a total of 1st 5½lb. Lastly, Rodney lost an extraordinary further 9lb to lose a total of 2st 1lb. And their cumulative weight loss came out at 7st 5½lb over the eight-week trial period. It was all very exciting.

But it wasn't just the weight that they had lost. Sally had enjoyed the most amazing inch losses, losing 6in from her bust, 7in from her waist and 7in from her hips plus 9in from her widest part, just above her thighs. But she was most shocked (and thrilled) that she had lost more than 3in from around each of her knees!

Angela lost a total of 20in – from her bust, waist, hips, tops of arms and thighs and her knees – while the men lost most weight from around their waist, with Rodney losing 5in, down from 44in to a trim 39in. Zena lost most of her inches from around her hips, down from 44in to 40in.

The overwhelming comment that came through from my famous five was that they really didn't feel hungry on the diet. It was this that I wanted to find out. Because this diet was based largely on high-fibre foods with a low Gi rating, it **should** help prevent hunger pangs and it did.

What the other dieters said

I soon started receiving completed questionnaires from the wider trial team of Radio Leicester listeners. There were 35 of them in total.

Vivienne Bland wrote:

'I was amazed at how easy the diet was to follow and I now weigh less than I have in the last 10 years. My goal was to be nearer 9st than 10st and I have achieved this.'

Diana Goodall, who lost 6lb in the first two weeks and a total of 1st 3lb in eight weeks, wrote:

'I have never previously drunk water [as a drink] and I am sure it has helped me to lose the weight. I hope to keep up this good habit. Other people have noticed that I have lost weight. I haven't been this weight for years, so thank you very, very much for letting me take part in this trial.'

Diana also sent me a label from some new trousers she had just bought. She wrote:

'These are a size less than I usually buy. I've always been thunder thighs so I have now had the label framed in my hall as it says, "Slim Leg!"'

In the questionnaire I asked if the dieters had experienced any health benefits since following the diet. An astonishing 94 per cent said they did feel healthier. One dieter, Jan Wiggins, commented that she had suffered fewer migraines since following the diet. Other trial dieters described some of the changes they had experienced.

Mrs Irene N. lost 1st 4lb in the eight-week trial and wrote:

'I would like to tell you the difference your diet has made to my life. I had a knee replacement four years ago, then in February this year I had a nasty fall. My knee was very swollen and badly bruised. I was only able to walk with crutches, and then walking sticks. The only time I went out was to the hospital for physiotherapy. I lost my confidence, felt very low and at the same time my doctor took me off HRT.

'My family were worried about me as I didn't want to talk or show any interest in anything. I heard you on the radio and applied. I am now a different lady! More energy, healthier, and feel much younger. My doctor is really pleased and so is my family. I used to go out in a big, long cardigan but now I am two dress sizes smaller and very happy to go out in a skirt and short-sleeved T-shirt. I can't thank you enough. I am a new woman at 63! Thank you very much.'

Irene also commented that after the second day she felt dreadful with a bad headache.

> 'It was as if I was having a healing crisis, like withdrawal symptoms from all the food I used to eat. By day four I was fine and I never looked back. I have more energy, confidence, and my general health is very good. The difference to my legs is tremendous. I am walking much better.'

Sue Newman lost 1st over the eight weeks, during which time she was away for a week with 3000 girl guides, camping in a field and in need of more calories to cope with the extra activity. Sue wrote:

> 'In the past if I had no weight loss I gave up. On this diet I jumped from no weight loss to loads but my dress size was getting smaller all the time so I carried on! My weight loss was from my whole body and I now have a "fat" bag with clothes in! All my colleagues and family have supported me in this – and that has never happened before – because I was eating healthy food, not on a "diet". My energy levels have gone up, my self-esteem has improved and my sex life is wonderful.'

Mr J. H. lost 12lb on the two-week Kick-start Diet and 1st 7lb in eight weeks as well as 4in from his chest and 4½in from his waist. He wrote:

> 'Although I enjoyed my holiday and tried to keep to the diet as close as possible I didn't gain any weight. I do

wonder what the total effect would have been if I had not gone away. The effect on my general health is so good I intend to carry on with stage two and achieve my ideal BMI [Body Mass Index] and try to sustain it.'

Phillip Waite lost 11lb in the first two weeks and 1st 8lb in eight weeks, with an impressive total inch loss of 23½. Phillip wrote:

'I feel that the diet has completely changed my life. It has taught me to think about the food that I eat and also the amount that I eat. Because I am much slimmer I am no longer embarrassed to go swimming and regularly swim half a mile. I also do a three-mile run four times a week. Without exercise I would not have lost as much weight. I now feel so much healthier and happier and intend to lose further weight. Thank you.'

Phillip's wife, Cheryl, also wrote:

'I wanted to say a big thank you to you and your trial diet. I went on the diet with Phillip because he desperately wanted to succeed and I thought it would help if I joined him. I also wanted to lose weight for our holiday in August.

'I was 10st 3lb and now weigh in at 9st 3lb. I am delighted and so surprised at how easy it was. I joined one of your diet and fitness classes and I am really enjoying the exercise class and hope to maintain the weight loss with the regular weigh-in sessions.'

Mrs C. P. lost 1st 10lb during the eight-week trial and wrote:

'Thank you, Rosemary. My blood pressure is down and my energy level is up. I'm sure it has made a big difference to my cholesterol levels also. I also lost a further 2lb in week nine, so I'm hoping for 2st off by week 10! My uniform for work looks great and I have a size "small" pair of jeans! I have more energy and feel happy with myself.'

Here is a summary of the trial results:

The average weight loss per person in the first two weeks was 7.25lb.
The average weight loss per person over the eight weeks was 1st 1.6lb.

When you realise that these folk were a random group of people all getting on with their lives, going on holiday (the trial was done over July and August), for them to achieve **an average weight loss of almost 2lb per week is amazing**! In previous trials of my other diets the best result was 1½lb per week and I thought that was good!

The resounding message that shone through as a difference with this diet was the fact that the diet satisfied the dieters. Even on the strict and lower-calorie Kick-start Diet a surprising 58 per cent said they didn't feel hungry at all or hardly ever, with 41 per cent saying they felt hungry only occasionally. Only one dieter said they were hungry often. On the more generous Part 2 of the diet 74 per cent said they were less hungry than on other diets, with 20 per cent saying they were slightly less hungry. (Not everyone answered this question as not everyone had been on a diet previously.)

Liz Biggs wrote:

'Thank you! Thank you . . . a diet that I think I can live with! Yes I've tried every diet under the sun (including your early ones) and managed to lose weight on most of them, but I was either hungry most of the time or they weren't a long-term sensible way of eating.

'I must admit to being disappointed when I first read the eating plan. It didn't seem particularly different and I was concerned about the amount of carbohydrates, having been an Atkins follower for a time. On closer inspection there seemed so much to eat, even on the Kick-start, that I thought I'd been sent some sort of non-diet that would be used as a comparison to the real one. However, the weight started to drop and I was convinced.

'Exercising is not something that I've done much of and so I thought that walking would be a safe and relatively painless option. I've worn out one pedometer, put the second in the wash and am awaiting the third! I'd like to start jogging but have too many wobbly bits and feel slightly ridiculous and very self-conscious. At the moment I content myself with jogging to crossroads during my walks around the village in the hope that people who see me will assume I'm in a hurry.

'I've still got a way to go. I hope to be at a healthy weight by Christmas and am feeling more optimistic and confident than I've felt for a long time.'

Liz lost 9lb in the first two weeks and 1st 10lb over eight weeks. She lost 2in from each thigh, 3in from her hips and 4in from around her abdomen plus 5in each off her waist and bust. Well done, Liz!

I asked my trial dieters if they had been on a diet prior to starting this one and 60 per cent of them had. This is quite significant as people often lose more weight at the start of a diet and then progress becomes slower. To jump from one diet straight on to another and see results like these is extraordinary.

I also asked the trial dieters if they had followed the exercise recommendations. The team did well: 25 per cent of them had exercised daily with their average weight loss totalling a staggering 1st 5lb over the eight weeks; 42 per cent had exercised for 20–30 minutes on five days a week and 23 per cent managed it three to four times a week. Only 6 per cent could only manage once or twice a week and these were people who had medical reasons for not being able to do more. I think the most encouraging thing for me to read was that 80 per cent of the dieters said they felt fitter and 65 per cent had seen an improvement in their body shape.

Pauline Sloan wrote:

'Because I have a ruptured tendon in my ankle I am unable to exercise as I would wish – walking all but short distances is out of the question and then only slowly.

'I am delighted to say that in the eight weeks I have lost 1st 9lb – the thrill of seeing "15" on the scales is magic! Apart from this I feel I have changed my eating habits and my attitude to what I eat.

'I used the chair exercise from your Ultimate Whole Body workout video whenever I could. I have also developed my own way of exercising, using the bed instead of the floor. And I am pleased to have lost the weight even though my movements were limited. I hope this will be of encouragement to anyone else with limited mobility.'

Losing weight is an easy measure of our progress on a weight-loss diet and fitness programme but there is nothing more motivating than to see the inches disappear. I asked if the dieters were surprised at their inch losses and 80 per cent said they were, 8.5 per cent said they weren't particularly surprised and 6 per cent said they weren't surprised.

With much of the diet being based on low-Gi foods, there was significantly more fibre included than in my previous eating plans. I wondered how dieters would cope with this so I asked them. I was surprised that 88 per cent admitted that they actually enjoyed it with 6 per cent saying they didn't mind it and another 6 per cent saying they were able to cope! I wondered if they felt they would be able to live with this type of diet in the longer term and I was delighted when 83 per cent said they certainly would, with the remaining 17 per cent saying they probably would do so.

Of course, one of the main features of this diet is that you are allowed a daily treat of anything you like within the 100-calorie limit and that it can be saved up for bigger treats if wished. I was interested to learn how important, or not, the treat was to my trial team. Of the trial team 42 per cent ate their treat every day while 16.5 per cent saved them up. Surprisingly, 34 per cent only had them occasionally and 8.5 per cent didn't eat them at all.

Joan Hillsdon lost 7lb on the Kick-start Diet and 1st 4lb in eight weeks. Joan wrote:

> 'Over the years losing weight hasn't been such a problem. However, since putting on 2½st three years ago it has been very difficult to lose even a pound – I thought it was my age, 60 years – but now I realise low fat and no white bread is the answer for me. Hiking and gardening are my hobbies so with only a little more exercise I feel very fit. Even my headaches and migraines are less frequent. The dinners are very good and so tasty and filling. The snacks seem too good to be true and I have never had chocolate on a diet before!'

So what about alcohol? Dieters are allowed 100 calories-worth of alcohol each day if they wish but 42 per cent of my dieters chose not to drink, 41 per cent drank only occasionally and surprisingly only 8.5 per cent said they drank every day.

Many folk are 'serial dieters' and I thought it would be interesting to find out a little of the dieting history of my team. For 11.5 per cent it was their first attempt at losing weight and 51 per cent had dieted occasionally but 37 per cent admitted that they had tried more diets than they cared to remember!

Binge eating is something that I experienced many years ago and it was the main reason for my own 2½st weight gain. Fortunately, I have been able to cure myself from bingeing, so maintaining my weight is much easier now, but I remember the anxiety it caused me for years. I am only too aware that many people still suffer with this problem so I asked my trial dieters to share their experiences.

While 22 per cent said they had never binged, 45 per cent

said they did occasionally while 28 per cent admitted that they often binged. So, I asked them how they had managed while following the trial diet. Taking only those who had binged before, only 3 per cent had continued to do so during the trial, with only 14 per cent admitting to doing so occasionally, but an impressive 83 per cent didn't binge at all.

I also asked the members of the team who had followed diets in the past if they had been more successful on this one than previously. A gratifying 83 per cent said they had been. So what was different? What did they like most about this diet?

I offered ten reasons why they might have liked it and asked them to tick the ones that they thought were most important for them. This is the result and, remember, they could tick more than one.

I didn't feel hungry on the diet	51%
I liked the food suggested	51%
I didn't feel it was like a diet	48%
It was easier to follow	45%
Counting the calories from each meal was easier than doing so for individual foods	34%
It offered more freedom of choice	31%
I could eat so much more than on previous diets	25%
It was good to be able to have a treat	25%
I could have a drink and not feel guilty	17%
The Power Snacks helped me not to cheat	17%

As one lady on the trial, who didn't want to be named, wrote:

'I have never eaten so much, so there was no time to be hungry!'

I hope you, too, will be able to enjoy similar benefits to your general health and fitness as a result of following this Gi Jeans Diet programme. I know that if you follow it you will change your life for the better and I hope that when you adopt the principles of this eating plan into your everyday lifestyle, you will never look back. Life is very, very good. Let's enjoy it to the full!

EXERCISE PLANNER

	M	T	W	T	F	S	S

MORNING SESSION

Aerobic workout
30 minutes ☐ ☐ ☐ ☐ ☐ ☐ ☐

Toning programme
10 minutes ☐ ☐ ☐ ☐ ☐ ☐ ☐

LUNCHTIME SESSION

Aerobic workout
30 minutes ☐ ☐ ☐ ☐ ☐ ☐ ☐

Toning programme
10 minutes ☐ ☐ ☐ ☐ ☐ ☐ ☐

AFTERNOON/ EVENING SESSION

Aerobic workout
30 minutes ☐ ☐ ☐ ☐ ☐ ☐ ☐

Toning programme
10 minutes ☐ ☐ ☐ ☐ ☐ ☐ ☐

WEIGHT AND INCH LOSS RECORD CHART

Date	My weight today	Weight loss to date	Inches/cm lost to date	Notes

Basal Metabolic Rate (BMR) Table

Women aged 18–29

Body Weight		BMR
Stones	Kilos	
7	45	1147
7.5	48	1194
8	51	1241
8.5	54	1288
9	57	1335
9.5	60.5	1382
10	64	1430
10.5	67	1477
11	70	1524
11.5	73	1571
12	76	1618
12.5	80	1665

Women aged 30–59

Body Weight		BMR
Stones	Kilos	
7	45	1208
7.5	48	1233
8	51	1259
8.5	54	1285
9	57	1311
9.5	60.5	1337
10	64	1373
10.5	67	1389
11	70	1414
11.5	73	1440
12	76	1466
12.5	80	1492

Women aged 60–74

Body Weight		BMR
Stones	Kilos	
7	45	1048
7.5	48	1073
8	51	1099
8.5	54	1125
9	57	1151
9.5	60.5	1176
10	64	1202
10.5	67	1228
11	70	1254
11.5	73	1279
12	76	1305
12.5	80	1331

13	83	1357	13	83	1518	13	83	1712
13.5	86	1382	13.5	86	1544	13.5	86	1760
14	89	1408	14	89	1570	14	89	1807
14.5	92	1434	14.5	92	1595	14.5	92	1854
15	95.5	1460	15	95.5	1621	15	95.5	1901
15.5	99	1485	15.5	99	1647	15.5	99	1948
16	102	1511	16	102	1673	16	102	1995
16.5	105	1537	16.5	105	1699	16.5	105	2043
17	108	1563	17	108	1725	17	108	2090
17.5	111	1588	17.5	111	1751	17.5	111	2137
18	115	1614	18	115	1776	18	115	2184
18.5	118	1640	18.5	118	1802	18.5	118	2231
19	121	1666	19	121	1828	19	121	2278
19.5	124	1691	19.5	124	1854	19.5	124	2325
20	127	1717	20	127	1880	20	127	2373

Basal Metabolic Rate (BMR) Table

Men aged 18–29			Men aged 30–59			Men aged 60–74		
Body Weight			Body Weight			Body Weight		
Stones	Kilos	BMR	Stones	Kilos	BMR	Stones	Kilos	BMR
7	45	1363	7	45	1384	7	45	1232
7.5	48	1411	7.5	48	1421	7.5	48	1270
8	51	1459	8	51	1457	8	51	1307
8.5	54	1507	8.5	54	1494	8.5	54	1345
9	57	1555	9	57	1530	9	57	1383
9.5	60.5	1602	9.5	60.5	1567	9.5	60.5	1421
10	64	1650	10	64	1603	10	64	1459
10.5	67	1698	10.5	67	1640	10.5	67	1497
11	70	1746	11	70	1676	11	70	1535
11.5	73	1794	11.5	73	1713	11.5	73	1573
12	76	1842	12	76	1749	12	76	1611
12.5	80	1890	12.5	80	1786	12.5	80	1649

13	83	1938	13	83	1822	13	83	1687
13.5	86	1986	13.5	86	1859	13.5	86	1725
14	89	2034	14	89	1895	14	89	1763
14.5	92	2082	14.5	92	1932	14.5	92	1801
15	95.5	2129	15	95.5	1968	15	95.5	1839
15.5	99	2177	15.5	99	2005	15.5	99	1877
16	102	2225	16	102	2041	16	102	1915
16.5	105	2273	16.5	105	2078	16.5	105	1953
17	108	2321	17	108	2114	17	108	1991
17.5	111	2369	17.5	111	2151	17.5	111	2028
18	115	2417	18	115	2187	18	115	2066
18.5	118	2465	18.5	118	2224	18.5	118	2104
19	121	2513	19	121	2260	19	121	2142
19.5	124	2561	19.5	124	2297	19.5	124	2180
20	127	2609	20	127	2333	20	127	2218

Index

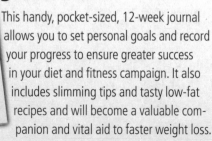

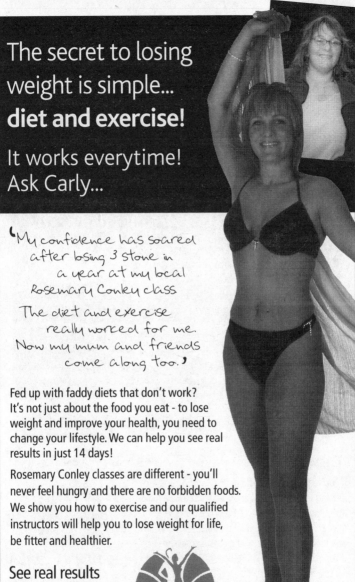

 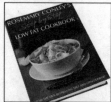